MORE THAN
SYMPATHY

Also by Steven D. Price

Teaching Riding at Summer Camp (The Stephen Greene Press, 1972)

Panorama of American Horses (Westover/Crown, 1973)

Civil Rights, Vols. 1 and 2 (Facts On File, 1973)

Get A Horse!: Basics of Backyard Horsekeeping (Viking, 1974)

Take Me Home: The Rise of Country-and-Western Music (Praeger, 1974)

The Second-Time Single Man's Survival Handbook, with William J. Gordon (Praeger, 1975)

Old as the Hills: The Story of Bluegrass Music (Viking, 1975)

Horseback Vacation Guide (The Stephen Greene Press, 1975)

Schooling to Show: Basics of Hunter-Jumper Training, with Anthony D'Ambrosio, Jr. (Viking, 1978)

The Whole Horse Catalog, Editorial Director (Simon & Schuster, 1979, revised 1985, 1993, 1998)

The Complete Book of Horse and Saddle Equipment, with Elwyn Hartley Edwards, (Quarto/Exeter, 1981)

Riding's a Joy, with Joy Slater (Doubleday, 1982)

All the King's Horses: The Story of the Budweiser Clydesdales (Viking, 1983)

The Beautiful Baby Naming Book (Simon & Schuster, 1984)

Riding for a Fall (Tor Books, 1988)

The Polo Primer, with Charles Kauffman (The Stephen Greene Press, 1989)

The Ultimate Fishing Guide (HarperCollins, 1996)

Caught Me A Big 'Un, with Jimmy Houston (Pocket Books, 1996)

The Complete Book of the American Quarter Horse (The Lyons Press, 1998)

Two Bits' Book of the American Quarter Horse (The Lyons Press, 1999)

The Quotable Horse Lover (The Lyons Press, 1999)

Essential Riding (The Lyons Press, 2000)

The Illustrated Horseman's Dictionary (The Lyons Press, 2000)

The Greatest Horse Stories Ever Told (The Lyons Press, 2001)

Classic Horse Stories (The Lyons Press, 2002)

1001 Smartest Things Ever Said (The Lyons Press, 2004)

1001 Dumbest Things Ever Said (The Lyons Press, 2004)

1001 Insults, Put-Downs, and Comebacks (The Lyons Press, 2005)

1001 Funniest Things Ever Said (The Lyons Press, 2006)

The Best Advice Ever Given (The Lyons Press, 2006)

1001 Best Things Ever Said about Horses (The Lyons Press, 2006)

1001 Best Things Ever Said about California (The Lyons Press, 2007)

The Horseman's Dictionary, Revised Edition, with Jessie Shiers (The Lyons Press, 2007)

The Quotable Billionaire (Skyhorse Publishing, 2009)

What to do When a Loved One Dies (Skyhorse Publishing, 2009)

The World's Funniest Lawyer Jokes (Skyhorse Publishing, 2011)

Endangered Phrases (Skyhorse Publishing, 2011)

Excuses for All Occasions (Skyhorse Publishing, 2012)

The Little Black Book of Writer's Wisdom (Skyhorse Publishing, 2013)

MORE THAN SYMPATHY

Essential Advice on Funerals, Money, Family, and Grief After the Death of a Loved One

Steven D. Price

Skyhorse Publishing

Skyhorse Publishing books may be purchased in bulk at special discounts for sales promotion, corporate gifts, fund-raising, or educational purposes. Special editions can also be created to specifications. For details, contact the Special Sales Department, Skyhorse Publishing, 307 West 36th Street, 11th Floor, New York, NY 10018 or info@skyhorsepublishing.com.

Skyhorse® and Skyhorse Publishing® are registered trademarks of Skyhorse Publishing, Inc.®, a Delaware corporation.

Visit our website at www.skyhorsepublishing.com.

10 9 8 7 6 5 4 3 2 1

Library of Congress Cataloging-in-Publication Data is available on file.

ISBN: 978-1-62636-427-1

Printed in the United States of America

Disclaimer: Nothing in this book should be construed to offer medical or legal advice and nothing contained herein is intended to be a substitute for qualified medical care provided by a physician or health care professional or legal and financial counsel provided by an attorney, paralegal, tax advisor, financial advisor, or certified public accountant.

To the Memory of My Parents

Cast a cold eye
On life, on death.
Horseman, pass by!
                    —William Butler Yeats

Contents

Acknowledgments

Many generous and thoughtful suggestions and contributions by the following people enhanced this book:

Laurence I. Burd, MD; Jeffrey A. Buckner, MD; Michael Cohen; Sue M. Copeland; Margaret Danson Gries; Sue Kessler Feld; Norman Fine; Jennifer Meyers Forsberg; Rabbi Eric Eisenkramer; Lesli Groves; Jonathan Leshanski, DVM; Beverly Wolf MacMahon; Jacqueline McQuade of the Schuyler Hill Funeral Home; Betsy Parker; Anne L. W. Price; John Sands; Mitchell Sweet, MD; and John Thornton.

I am equally grateful to Ruth Mechaneck, PhD and to C. Toni Mufson, MSW, for their perceptive assistance on the grief counseling and therapy chapter; to Anthony Ard, Esq., for his review of the legal aspects of the text, to Nick Lyons for his editorial scrutiny and guidance, to Tony Lyons for suggesting the project, and to the Skyhorse staff, and especially Abigail R. Gehring, for helping to bring this book to fruition.

You Step Forward

> *"You give but little when you give of your possessions. It is when you give of yourself that you truly give."*
>
> **—Kahlil Gibran**

Death comes in many forms, at many ages, and in many ways. Some are anticipated; death at an advanced age is the logical consequence of life. Death from a terminal disease does not come as a complete surprise, either, and is especially sad when a young person is involved, but is also inevitable.

Then there are unanticipated deaths. The phone rings or someone comes to the door—a relative, friend, medical authorities, the police, or the military—and you are informed that a loved one has been killed in an auto accident or plane crash or was the victim of a crime of violence or a casualty of war. If any death can be called more devastating than others, that one may be suicide, and learning of the death is harder still if you are the person who discovers it.

You and the deceased's other near and dear ones will be horrified, shocked, or in denial, but as the reality sinks in, you ask yourself, "Now what?"

To say that death isn't a pleasant topic is beyond understatement, and the inclination to retreat from its grim face is a very natural human response. Nevertheless, the very inevitability of the end of life no matter by what cause or at what age should help to make us face the unavoidable. Rather than retreating in denial or fear or squeamishness, stepping forward to help make the necessary funeral arrangements and then to help sort out the financial and emotional aftermath is an act of kindness—indeed, of love—to the deceased and to all others who mourn.

That person is you. We'll call you "the representative" because you've agreed to represent the next of kin's best interests and—in a very real sense—your loved one's, too. We can assume that you have stepped forward to be such a guiding force, a "quarterback," a "strong hand on the tiller," or however else you choose to characterize your role. The deceased may be someone with no other friends or relatives, although he or she is more likely to be a parent, a child, a close relative, or dear friend. He or she may have had other relatives and friends who might have been closer than you, but because of your willingness, the other mourners/survivors gratefully accept your offer.

Although this book is organized in the chronological order in which events following a death usually occur, the information found in certain chapters may become relevant earlier or later—out of order, so to speak. For example, probate proceedings may begin before a memorial service takes place, or grief therapy may be called for even before the funeral. Accordingly, let me suggest that you familiarize yourself with all the subjects covered in these pages so you'll have a panoramic view of what to do when a loved one dies.

CHAPTER 1

The Death

> *"Death does not blow a trumpet."*
>
> **—Danish proverb**

The legal formalities and practical decisions surrounding a death will depend on when, where, and how it occurred.

In the case of an anticipated death at home, a doctor in attendance will sign a death certificate identifying the deceased and stating the time, place, and cause of death (other items will be filled in by the funeral director at a later time). If the death happens at home and someone phones the 911 emergency number, the responding ambulance will notify the police. If no one else was there at the time of death, the police must come to determine whether there might have been foul play (in some jurisdictions, the police are also eligible to fill out a death certificate).

Depending on local law, the body may have to be taken to a hospital or morgue for a formal pronouncement of death. If not, the body may be taken to a funeral home, although in most places the body cannot be removed until a doctor or medical examiner signs a death certificate.

When the death happens at a hospital, whether or not the deceased had been a patient—for example, if the deceased was taken there as the result of a traffic or crime fatality—an attending emergency-room physician will sign the death certificate. The body will be held pending instructions with regard to where it is to be moved. The same procedure applies to a nursing home or hospice situation.

Deaths that occur out of state or in another country and in connection with military service will be discussed in the next chapter.

Municipalities and most states require autopsies to determine or confirm certain causes of death. As a general rule, an examination is called for after a death by violence, suicide, accident, or drug or alcohol overdose. Deaths that occur in prison or from an employment-related injury may also be grounds, as is a catchall "while in apparent good health" category. In addition, relatives may request an autopsy for their own edification when the exact reason for the death is unclear. The autopsy is performed at a hospital or morgue, and how quickly the procedure can be completed will depend on how quickly a hospital pathologist or the municipality's medical examiner's office (some places call it the coroner's office) can get to it.

NOTIFYING OTHERS

Your role as representative begins when you start notifying people. That job requires recollection, research, and organization, so get out a pad and pencil or turn on your computer and make a list of everyone who will want to know about the death of—let's personalize the circumstances by referring to the deceased as Uncle Fred. The list will include relatives, friends, neighbors, employers and business associates, former business associates, former neighbors—in short, just about everyone. If you can locate Uncle Fred's address book (including his computer's e-mail addresses) or Christmas card list, so much the better.

Whether or not you were close to Uncle Fred, the next step is read the list to someone who knew him well enough to know whether you left anyone out. There might be a long-lost cousin with whom Uncle Fred reestablished contact without your knowing about it or a favorite waiter at the diner where he had breakfast several times a week (and if that was his habit, you'd certainly want to break the news to the diner's owner).

Next, narrow the list down to those who should know immediately. Notification is an emotionally draining process, especially when a death was unexpected. Besides, people will ask whether there will be a service and, if so, when it will take place; until you know those details, there's no reason to have to tell everyone that you'll be back in touch.

Although notification in person or by telephone is the most personal way and by written correspondence the most traditional, the widespread use of the Internet has made e-mail, even instant messaging, an acceptable method if older recipients won't be offended by electronic communication. Rather than spring the sad news on the unwary in the body of the text, you might give advance warning on the "subject" line with "very sad news about Uncle Fred."

Another way to notify the world is via social networks like Facebook, Twitter, and MySpace. If you're not a member, ask people who are—find them by asking around, especially teenagers and young adults—to send the news to other members who knew the deceased. Many belong to specialized groups that the loved one belonged to—high school or college classmates, summer camp alumni, military units, fans of pop musicians, bass fishermen—where a note can be posted.

If Uncle Fred had been working, his employer should immediately be notified unless, of course, the death occurred on the job. Get the name of someone in the company's human resources department whom you'll want to ask at some point—but not now—about any money that might be due, including compensation for outstanding vacation or sick time, and any survivor benefits, such as a company-issued life insurance policy. Also make a note to get in touch with any unions and other professional or service organizations with regard to life insurance or other benefits, including—and especially—funeral coverage.

LOCATING DOCUMENTS AND SECURING THE PROPERTY

Locating a copy of the Will (the word is customarily capitalized to distinguish it from the future-tense "will") is a particularly important first step, since the document may contain instructions about funeral arrangements. Even if it does not, Uncle Fred may have written a "to be opened in the event of my death" letter bundled together with the Will. The most likely place to find it will be a home safe or strongbox, a bank safe-deposit box, or especially with Uncle Fred's lawyer. The lawyer, it goes without saying, should be one of the first people you notify, since gaining access to a deceased person's safe-deposit box may require some legal assistance. If the deceased had a lawyer but you don't know who it is, look in the Will or Uncle Fred's address book, or ask one of his relatives.

There may also be an organ donor card or certificate (driver's licenses also have such instructions). Even if the family objects to donations, the provisions must be complied with. There may also be a power of attorney document that will entitle someone to act on the deceased's behalf in certain ways.

If Uncle Fred lived alone or if all the occupants of a house died in a car crash or other common disaster, certain details call for immediate attention. Placing minor children with a guardian or another caregiver until the matter of custody is decided is the highest priority.

Pets are like children to many people who live alone. What to do with a surviving pet can be as easy as giving the dog, cat, or bird to someone who knows and loves the animal or as difficult as giving it to an animal rescue organization or pet shelter. Don't assume, however, that every rescue organization or shelter will accept every pet, especially an older or an infirm one; a veterinarian advises that a financial "endowment" to cover inevitable medical expenses would make the animal a more welcome guest.

Although you'll want to keep the phone and electricity on until the place is sold or rented, stop any newspaper delivery, magazine subscription, and health or social club membership right away; the deceased's estate may be entitled to a refund on the unused portion of a subscription or contract. Any daily home care or "Meals on Wheels" or a daily or weekly house-keeper should also be discontinued. If you can find the person's calendar, look for medical and other appointments that should be canceled.

Credit cards should be canceled, too. Contact the issuers to inform them of the death and to make sure that no one can use the card under the deceased person's name (charges and any unpaid balance will be paid by the estate). Some cards include a life insurance policy, so inquire about that possibility.

An empty house or apartment invites prowlers, some of whom routinely scan obituary pages for likely places to hit. If there is no house- or apartment-sitter, set some of the lights on a timer.

Be sure to remove wallets, purses, checkbooks and bank passbooks, watches and other jewelry, and small antiques and other valuables. Even if there will be no prowlers, there will be traffic through the residence, strangers as well as familiar faces, and Oscar Wilde's oft-quoted line, "I can resist everything but temptation," is applicable here. However, access to the premises may be difficult or legally impossible, depending on the nature of the death; apartments and houses are sometimes sealed by the police pending searches and investigations.

Clean out the refrigerator of milk and other perishables.

A trustworthy neighbor or the apartment's superintendent can collect and hold the mail, or it can be held at the post office. The local police should be notified that a house is now vacant, so that passing patrol cars can be alerted to any suspicious activity. To give the place a "lived-in" look, arrange to have the lawn mowed in the spring and summer, leaves raked in the fall, and sidewalk and front doorway shoveled in winter.

Also with regard to security, burglars scan obituary notices on the prospect that a house will be vacant during the funeral, so having a relative, friend, or neighbor who isn't keen about attending funerals there to guard the house or apartment isn't a bad idea.

Other people try to take advantage of recent deaths. People store property in apartment house basements, and superintendents and landlords don't always see fit to direct a deceased's survivors to those items. "Estate purchasers" have been known to appear as soon as they learn of a likely situation; some are even notified by the police as soon as a death occurs. Taking advantage of an emotionally vulnerable moment, the would-be buyer looks around as much of the residence as he can, then offers a lowball figure for everything. "My truck is downstairs," the grieving survivors are told, "and I'm not coming back—take it or leave it."

And, alas, that's often the first of other hustles and scams (about which we talk later).

The death of a person who lives alone brings to mind a story that some say is apocryphal, but, as it was supposed to have occurred in New York City, where anything can happen, so it may well be true.

For reasons too complicated to go into here, New York has real estate laws that keep the rents of many older apartments well below market prices. Finding and getting such an apartment is a prize; wars have been fought for less.

The resident of such an apartment house returned home one day to find the building's superintendent coming out of a neighboring apartment with two policemen and a medical examiner's office team. On a stretcher was a bag holding the apartment's occupant who had just died.

The resident quickly phoned a friend. "So-and-so just died. He was a bachelor. Here's the landlord's phone number. Call now and take the apartment!"

The friend phoned back within five minutes. "Too late!"

"What do you mean—too late?" The neighbor replied. "The guy died not more than an hour ago."

"Too late," the friend repeated. "The landlord said that the medical examiner who pronounced the guy dead had called first—he took the apartment."

CHAPTER 2

The Funeral Home

> *"In the midst of life we are in death."*
>
> **—The Book of Common Prayer**

More often than not, the choice of funeral home will be almost preordained. Many small towns have only one, and indeed there are still places where only one serves an entire county. Even when there is a choice, some establishments have acquired a reputation as "the" place to use based on the deceased's family's race, faith, or national origin. Status, too, can be a determining factor: At least one New York City establishment prides itself on burying what's left of Society-with-a-capital-*S*.

In cases where the deceased had ties to a religious community, the church, synagogue, mosque, or other place of worship is likely to have an ongoing relationship with a funeral home, one that has served the congregation for generations (funeral homes tend to be a family affair) and that is run and staffed by people who may well have known the deceased.

If not, you or the next of kin may have attended a funeral at an establishment that you or they found comfortable and comforting, or you can ask around for recommendations.

WORKING WITH A FUNERAL DIRECTOR

The services of a funeral director are invaluable for handling details, a compelling argument against "do-it-yourself" funerals in which family and friends take on that role. The director has been trained and is experienced in every stage, from releasing the body from the hospital or coroner, preparing the body for burial or cremation, assisting in planning the memorial service, arranging for the cemetery to open the burial plot, and handling myriad other necessary legal and practical matters. Like life, death is complicated, especially when a loved one died in another state or—more intricate still—another country, or wanted to be buried abroad. When a loved one dies, quite frankly, there is no time for on-the-job training.

In the last stages of a terminal illness, you may have selected a funeral home and notified its director that the establishment's services will be needed. At that time, you may have been told to gather certain information in anticipation of the end, including vital statistics, provisions in a Will about the disposition of the person's remains, and cemetery location and the deed to the burial plot.

However, and far more likely, your initial contact with the director will be a phone call notifying him of the death and requesting the funeral home's services. The funeral director will then tell you what to bring when you two meet.

That meeting will be your first real exposure to paperwork. The funeral director will have obtained the death certificate, which must be completely filled out and filed with the municipality's department of health in order to obtain a burial permit. In addition to the deceased's full name, certain other information will be required, and you should have it available:

- The deceased's full name;
- Last residence, including city, state, and zip code (the hospital in which the patient died is not considered the residence);
- Date and place (city and state) of birth, gender, race, citizenship, and Social Security number;
- Marital status. If married, the surviving spouse's name must be included (if the wife, her maiden name must also be included, if it is different);
- Occupation. Most jurisdictions do not accept "retired"—the industry or type of business and the city and state where located must be given;
- If a veteran, the armed forces branch and the years of service;

- Father's first and last name, mother's first and maiden name; and
- The relationship of the person providing the information for the deceased.

In addition, the director will want any information with regard to a cemetery or other plans for the disposition of the remains and whether there will be a funeral.

RELOCATING THE REMAINS

Because the aftermath of a death places mourners is a time of emotional vulnerability and under certain time constraints, the Federal Trade Commission enacted regulations that help funeral directors offer and mourners receive fair dealings. You as representative will be given a written list of available goods and services, along with the price of each item. You will be told you are under no obligation to purchase ones you don't want. For a traditional funeral, those goods and services include transporting the body to and from the funeral home, use of the establishment's facilities for viewing and/or a funeral or memorial service, preparing the body (including embalming), a casket or urn, and a guest register and acknowledgment cards. As an educated consumer, you as representative should not agree to anything unless and until you feel comfortable with (another way of saying not intimidated by) everything on the itemized list that you have selected or are being asked to select. That involves knowing what sort of funeral or memorial service—or none at all—you and the next of kin will want, subjects we'll get to later in this chapter and also in the next chapter.

In most cases, the funeral home will retrieve the deceased from home or hospital. However, a death in another state will necessarily require additional arrangements, especially if local laws require an autopsy first. The funeral director will handle the necessary paperwork and arrange for transportation, whether by ground or air.

You may wish to travel to wherever the body is to provide emotional support to someone else who wants to go, and then accompany the body home. If so, and if air travel is involved, ask the airline or your travel agent whether a "compassion" or "bereavement" discount rate is available. You'll have to provide the airline with such proof of why you qualify as a copy of the death certificate and a funeral home or hospital contact. ("Compassion" rates also apply to mourners who are traveling to a funeral, so be sure to alert out-of-towners to their existence.)

A death in a foreign country is considerably more complicated. If Uncle Fred died while on a tour of southern Italy, for example, in the most straightforward of scenarios, local officials will notify our State Department's nearest consular official, who will in turn alert the Bureau of Consular Affairs in Washington, DC. That agency will locate and inform his next of kin or anyone else who is listed on his passport application. But if

Fred had been traveling alone and became separated from his passport, or he was a disaster victim and his remains couldn't be identified, the consulate's job becomes far more difficult.

In any event, the Bureau of Consular Affairs provides guidance to the family and the funeral director with regard to returning the remains to this country; it also arranges for such paperwork as documents to facilitate going through Customs. Despite what you might have heard, our government does not pay the cost of returning citizens who die abroad; the Bureau transmits to the embassy or consulate instructions and private funds to cover the costs involved. When the formalities are taken care of, the consular officer will send to the next of kin or legal representative a Foreign Service Report of Death, which is essential for settling estate matters. The officer will also return personal effects if desired, again at the family's expense.

The military has its own very specific protocols and procedures for returning bodies killed in action or while otherwise serving this country. The funeral director and a representative of the branch in which the deceased served will handle such matters. (See pages 41 to 43 for information on military burials and survivor benefits.)

Among questions the funeral director will have are:

- Will the body be embalmed? Embalming is primarily done to disinfect and preserve the remains, a matter of concern to funeral home employees and others who must handle them. Then, too, if there will be a wake or visitation with an open casket, most bodies change in appearance shortly after death, and embalming retards those biochemical changes. However, and contrary to popular belief, no laws require embalming except in such instances as shipment between states (although there can be exceptions for religious reasons) and after death from certain communicable diseases. The most compelling reason is when a funeral will take place more than several days after death, especially if there will be viewing and/or an open casket.

• Will the funeral have a closed or an open casket? If an open casket, in what clothing will the deceased be buried, and who will select the garment(s)? If there is to be cosmetic enhancement, especially after an accident or a disease that marred the deceased's face, the funeral home's cosmetician will welcome a recent color photo as a guide.

• Are there items with which the deceased wished or might have wished to be buried or cremated or that the survivors would like to see included? A photo of loved ones or a religious article such as a rosary or prayer book are typical, although almost anything else that's meaningful can be interred or cremated. A youngster who loved to play baseball was buried in his Little League uniform and with his mitt, while an amateur musician's casket included his trumpet and the sheet music of his favorite tune.

- Who, if anyone, will serve as a pallbearer? Six relatives and/or close friends who are physically able to lift and carry the casket is the traditional number, although those who cannot because of age or infirmity can be named honorary pallbearers. Otherwise, the funeral home will provide pallbearers, or the casket can be wheeled in and out of the place of worship or out of the funeral home.

- Who will conduct the service? A particular church, synagogue, mosque, or temple where the deceased worshipped would most likely be where he would have wanted the rites to be held and to be conducted by its spiritual leader. If not, funeral homes have chapels or easy access to them. A graveside service is another possibility, as is one held at a crematorium, if appropriate. The funeral director, who has undoubtedly worked with ministers, priests, rabbis, and imams in the community, can recommend a member of the clergy if you don't have one in mind.

- Will there be flowers? In addition to arrangements that many people send to the funeral home, you may want to order something special—if Uncle Fred was a big sports fan, a display in his favorite team's colors would not be inappropriate.

- Will transportation be necessary? In case there are more mourners than available space in private cars to and from the cemetery, as often happens with out-of-towners who do not come by car, the funeral home will arrange for limousines. That isn't one of the first things you need to discuss, but keep the matter in mind so you can give the funeral director enough advance notice if need be.

The funeral director will also want to know about the disposition of the remains: interment, entombment, or cremation.

- Interment, which refers to burying the deceased in the ground, is the most prevalent form of disposition of remains. If Uncle Fred had planned ahead and bought a plot, the funeral director will need the deed to arrange with the cemetery to open the grave (one of the fees included in the itemized list). A hearse will convey the casket to the cemetery from the funeral home or the place of worship where a service has been held, or directly to the cemetery if there is to be a graveside service. With mourners in attendance, a member of the clergy will typically conduct a brief service, whereupon the casket is lowered into the ground. In some traditions, mourners toss a symbolic shovelful of soil or a flower into the grave. After the mourners leave, cemetery workers complete the interment.

To ensure that gravesites are kept neat, cemeteries charge an annual maintenance fee. If Uncle Fred had made prior arrangements or if his survivors wish, a lump-sum perpetual care fee is an alternative to annual payments.

- Entombment is aboveground burial, most frequently in a mausoleum, an imposing stone or concrete building that contains more than one crypt (the individual space for a casket). Far more prevalent in the era of family togetherness, entombment is rarely done now, but if there is room in the family's mausoleum and the deceased had expressed a desire to be buried there, it remains an option. The casket is placed in its crypt, which is then sealed. A service can be conducted in the mausoleum, just as at a graveside funeral.

- Cremation: A steadily increasing number of

funerals involve cremation, a subject that deserves a fuller discussion than interment and entombment. Reasons include a belief that it is more "eco-friendly" than the other two methods, a wish to return "ashes to ashes and dust to dust," and a repugnance at the thought of one's body decaying in the ground.

The procedure takes place at a crematorium, also known as a *crematory*. Once the cremation chamber is heated, the body, usually encased in a cardboard or another disposable container, is placed into the chamber (embalming is not necessary). The entire procedure, including a cool-down period, takes between four and five hours, depending on the body's size and weight. "Ashes" is a somewhat misleading image, in that the remains, which are referred to as "cremains," look nothing like what a wood-burning fireplace produces. Light gray or white bone fragments pulverized to the consistency of coarse sand are all that remain (an average adult's ashes weigh about five pounds). These are gathered and placed in an urn that the next of kin have selected and purchased in advance.

Although pacemakers and medical infusion pumps, which are highly explosive, must be removed first, the deceased can wear jewelry.

However, since the intense heat is almost certain to melt the items, engagement and wedding rings and other highly personal effects are customarily removed prior to cremation and then placed with the remains in the urn afterward.

CREMATION VS. INTERMENT

A cremation service need not differ from an interment funeral, including a visitation in a place of worship or a funeral home followed by a funeral service; the deceased usually reposes in a rented casket and is usually embalmed if there is to be a viewing. Another choice is direct cremation, in which the deceased is taken from the place of death to the funeral home until paperwork is completed and then taken to the crematorium.

Cremation affords far more "burial" options than interment or entombment do. An urn may be interred in a cemetery plot or entombed in a mausoleum or a niche at a cemetery or crematorium. It may be buried on private property, where families often plant a memorial bush or tree or place a headstone to mark the site. Or it may be kept at home, sometimes prominently displayed.

Ashes are often scattered, sometimes in cemetery sections designated for that purpose, over private land with the owner's permission, or over public land or water subject to local regulations. If scattering the ashes at sea is an appealing idea and the family has no access to a boat, the funeral or crematorium director or many websites can arrange for charter boats or an airplane.

Macabre but practical is the advice to be mindful of wind speed and direction when scattering ashes. There may be other considerations, too. A friend whose aunt lived and died on Florida's west coast volunteered to scatter her ashes in the Gulf of Mexico at sunset, as she had wished. (*What do you wear for ashes-scattering, even on a beach?* he wondered, and, being a proper sort of man, he wore a dark suit that made him look, he said, like Nixon walking along the San Clemente beach.)

It turned out that a group of "Sundowners" congregated every evening at the secluded cove my friend had chosen. Nevertheless, among the wearers of Hawaiian shirts and sarongs quaffing margaritas and gin and tonics, he removed his shoes and socks and rolled up his pants legs and waded into the surf. As he removed the urn cover, he had a moment of dismay: "I should have checked the tide chart," he panicked. If the tide were coming in, Auntie's ashes would spend eternity among driftwood, seaweed, clamshells and other beach detritus. But, fortunately, the tide was ebbing, so Auntie went right out to sea.

One nonfuneral option is body donation. Contrary to popular opinion, a person or his or her survivors don't sell the body to a medical school; the only cost is likely to be for transporting the body to the institution. Some schools require that an individual enroll in a body donor program before his or her death, but other schools allow the next of kin to make the decision after their loved one's death. After medical study, the remains are usually cremated and can be returned to the family. Not all bodies are acceptable, however; obesity and certain diseases are reasons for rejection.

DRAFTING AN OBITUARY

A newspaper obituary or death notice is customary, and the funeral director will be able to place the item for you. He will also be able to furnish the cost per column inch as well as the cost of a photograph if you want one to accompany the text.

Strictly speaking, an obituary is a brief statement of facts: the person's name; age; date and place of death; cause of death (optional); names of spouse and children; names of siblings, nephews, nieces, and other close relatives; names of predeceased relatives; location and day and time of funeral (or "private funeral service" or "interment private" or "memorial service at a date to be announced"); location of cemetery if there will be a burial; location of any reception afterward; and name of any organization to whom donations may be made.

Adjectives of endearment preceding the names of survivors are traditional, so the obituary may read:

> GREEN, Fredrick, 88, of Hometown, passed away Sunday, December 13, at home of natural causes. Proud grandfather of Susan. Loving uncle of John, Sally,

Susan, and Joan. Predeceased by his adored wife Mary and beloved son Fredrick Jr. Services at 10:30 AM on Wednesday, December 16, at Hometown Community Church. Burial at Hometown Cemetery. In lieu of flowers, a donation to the American Red Cross would be appreciated.

A death notice is far more biographical. Where Uncle Fred went to school, his military service, his business experience, and membership in civic, fraternal, athletic, and other organizations would be mentioned, as well as any favorite hobbies or other activities, along the lines of:

GREEN, Fredrick 88, of Hometown, PA, passed away Sunday, December 13, at home of natural causes. Proud grandfather of Susan. Loving uncle of John and Joan. Predeceased by his adored wife Mary and beloved son Fredrick Jr.

After attending Hometown High and the University of Pennsylvania, Fred served in the army during World War II, during which he reached the rank of major and was awarded a Bronze Star. A leader in the automobile industry, he worked for several auto distributorships before opening his own Green Motors, from which he retired fifteen years ago. Fred was an active Rotarian and Hometown High Football Booster, and he loved fishing, bowling, watching old TV show reruns, visiting Susan and her friends in San Francisco, and taking long walks with his devoted cocker spaniel Spotty.

Services at 10:30 AM on Wednesday, December 16, at Hometown Community Church. Burial at

Hometown Cemetery. In lieu of flowers, a donation to
the American Red Cross would be appreciated.

Showing your draft of the obituary or death notice to
another person who knew the deceased is helpful in case you
missed or misstated anything.

Local newspapers will write and publish death notice articles
about longtime and/or prominent members of the community.
If the person achieved some degree of fame in a particular
activity, regional and national papers will also do so for, for
example, movie actors, authors, musicians, artists, politicians,
and athletes. The article will usually be written by someone
in the relevant department, such as a sports editor writing the
death notice of a retired major-league baseball player.

BUYING A CASKET OR URN

The casket or urn will be the most expensive single item, with
the likely exception of a cemetery plot. Consult the funeral
home's price list as you look over the choices, and bear in mind
that funeral directors have been known to show the more
expensive items first.

With regard to caskets, prices depend on the material
of which the casket is made, the lining, and the hardware.
The least expensive is usually fiberboard; more costly are
more substantially constructed caskets. The choice of wood
includes pine, walnut, cherry, mahogany, or oak. Unfinished

pine, which is usually the least expensive, is traditional for members of the Jewish faith. Caskets are also available in such hardwoods as ash, maple, elm, poplar, and cottonwood. Many are hand-sculpted and given a polished finish that adds both to the appearance and the cost.

Metal caskets are made of bronze, copper, or stainless steel. The first two are priced according to weight, while stainless-steel caskets are priced by their thickness.

No casket can preserve remains forever, and Federal Trade Commission regulations prohibit claiming that "sealed," "protective," and "gasketed" caskets conserve the body (all that seals and gaskets can do is keep the eventual seepage of moisture from the soil into the casket).

A casket's construction or appearance is not a factor for a cremation; the deceased will be placed in a simple cardboard, heavy fabric, or unfinished wooden box.

Until recently, caskets were sold only through funeral homes, but they are now available at showrooms that sell them and even over the Internet. Another FTC rule stipulates the funeral director may not refuse to accept a casket bought somewhere else and may not change a "handling" fee.

Urns come in a wide variety of shapes and sizes: marble and other stone, many varieties of wood and metal, glass, and ceramic. The urn can be plain or adorned, again depending on the deceased's preference if preordered or the family's. Like caskets, urns can be purchased over the Internet—websites offer "theme" urns: religious, patriotic, and just about every sport, hobby, and lifestyle (at least one site—www.memorial-urns. com—has an intriguing selection of "biker" urns).

CHAPTER 3

The Service

> *"I can't think of a more wonderful thanksgiving for the life*
> *I have had than that everyone should be jolly at my funeral."*
>
> **—Lord Louis Mountbatten**

At no time can religion offer greater comfort than at the death of a loved one. Most religions provide an emotional link to the deceased and the promise of a better afterlife to the faithful, and their rituals can embrace and support mourners at this most difficult time.

As a general rule, the more traditional the faith, the fewer choices that you as the representative planning the service will have. Tenets of orthodox religions prescribe every step of the process, from the care given to the body to postburial mourning periods and everything in between. Nevertheless, even very traditional funerals may have some flexibility with regard, for example, to the choice of liturgical music and readings. (See Appendix B for brief descriptions of the funeral practices of the major faiths.)

That's not to say that nonreligious mourners cannot derive just as much solace from observances of their own making. I have attended funerals and memorial services that made no mention of a Supreme Being or Life Everlasting; although "enjoyed" might not be the precise word to describe my reaction, I was impressed, moved—and comforted.

Not every death must be followed by a service. If Uncle Fred didn't want a funeral or memorial service, his wishes should be taken into account. He might have expressed them in his Will, a letter to be opened at his death, or in conversations. If there's no such direction or expression of intent, then the survivors' wishes will prevail, which often involve overriding the deceased's "no public mourning—just bury me" request in favor of some sort of ceremony. Or not—some survivors prefer no ceremony at all. A widow of my acquaintance insisted that her husband's remains go directly to the crematorium and then to the cemetery without anyone—including herself—in attendance. That's admittedly unusual, but one must defer to the next of kin's wishes, no matter how unusual.

A service can take the form of a funeral or a memorial service. The distinction is whether or not the deceased will be present: a funeral involves the person's remains, while a memorial service does not. Certain religions require funerals, but many permit choosing between the two types.

There can also be both. We've all heard about or perhaps attended funerals that have been privately held and were then followed weeks or even months later by a memorial service. That's especially true in the cases of public figures whose families wish a private interment in order to keep crowds away; a subsequent memorial service accommodates participants whose professional and travel schedules require planning far in advance, as well as giving them plenty of time to plan a eulogy or musical performance.

A third option is a graveside burial or a crematorium service, especially appropriate and practical for a limited number of mourners, such as an elderly person with few friends and relatives.

THE SERVICE: WHEN AND WHERE?

Religious doctrine often determines when the funeral will take place. For example, Judaism and Islam require a quick interment, often the day the person died, a tradition that goes back to the warm climate in the part of the world where those faiths arose. That timing may also be the preference of others, religious or not, who believe that earthly remains should be dealt with as soon as possible once a person's life has ended.

Many people see no need for such haste. Funerals may take place many days or even more than a week after death. Visitations or wakes are customary in such cases, held at either a funeral home or someone's—often the deceased's—residence. A newspaper or online obituary notice and word of mouth will spread the word about the time and place. Refreshments are customarily served, often provided by mourners who bring cakes, cookies, pies, and perhaps something more substantial. A large coffee urn and teapot, as well as plates and cups (paper or otherwise), and utensils and glasses (plastic or otherwise) will be essential. Many wakes or visitations display objects that relate to the deceased, such as photos, awards, and items from the person's career.

When relatives and friends who live a great distance away wish to attend the service, it is necessary to take their travel time into account. Don't forget to tell them about airline "compassion" fares, then, in your role of representative/coordinator, appoint someone to provide or help find accommodations for out-of-towners who need a place to stay. Another chore is to provide or hire babysitters for infants and children who are too young to attend the funeral.

MEMORIAL SERVICES

Memorial services over which a member of the clergy does not preside will require someone—a relative or friend of the deceased or perhaps you—to serve as a sort of master of ceremonies. That's no more than someone to offer opening remarks and then introduce the other participants. That person shouldn't be anyone who is likely to be overcome by grief; indeed, he or she should be prepared to offer emotional (and sometimes physical) support to speakers who falter during their remarks.

You'll want to give all the speakers plenty of time to prepare what they're going to say, although opening the floor to impromptu recollections is a warm and loving way to share grief (someone who went to such a memorial service described it as an "open mike night").

Memorial services are another occasion to display mementos. A table or easel—or both—might include family album photos, athletic event programs, trophies, or other prizes—anything that provides a nostalgic link. These mementos will also serve as conversation-starters among strangers, along the lines of, "Gee, I didn't know your Uncle Fred played college football." Items from the person's career are also fair game: A service for an author had a collection of dust jackets of the books she had written.

The death of a young person is always poignant, and an unexpected death even more so. Here's how a friend described such an occurrence:

> My nephew was extremely popular at the university
> he was attending, both as a soccer player and as

a member of the student body at large. When he collapsed and died during an evening pickup game of soccer (the ultimate diagnosis was hypertrophic cardiomyopathy), his teammates were devastated. They followed the emergency personnel to the hospital and kept begging the ER doc who worked on my nephew to go back and keep trying to revive him.

A candlelight vigil was held the day after his death, and hundreds attended—students, faculty, friends, and family. Student after student took the microphone to relate the positive impact my nephew had had on his or her life. On the following day, a special viewing of the body was arranged for the soccer team, so that they could say good-bye to their teammate and find some closure to this disorienting event.

My nephew died in California, where he was attending school; his funeral was held in Kentucky, where he grew up. Several team members flew to Kentucky to attend the funeral and participate in a bonfire party later that evening at his family's home. My brother-in-law has said the bonfire may become an annual event, open to anyone who wishes to gather to celebrate the memory of his son.

My sister and brother-in-law had indicated that, instead of flowers, well-wishers might contribute to their son's soccer team. That fund is now nearing $25,000, at which point it will become a perpetual endowment in my nephew's name. In tragedies like this, where people long to "do something," yet there's little to be done, a fund such as this can be highly cathartic. People feel that they're honoring the young person who has died, plus giving a measure of comfort to the grieving parents. It's not "enough," but it's something.

Above all, and whether a funeral or a memorial service, the occasion should reflect the deceased's life and spirit. Its setting and contents should be memorable in two ways: as an occasion to celebrate the memory of the departed and as an event that participants and audience will be happy to remember for years to come.

Almost any public space—a library, meeting hall, theater, or concert hall—will rent its facilities for a memorial service. So will a restaurant or a tavern that had some significance in Uncle Fred's life so that hours of toasts and anecdotes can echo off the wood-paneled walls. Fred may have belonged to a civic, athletic, or fraternal organization that will offer its lodge or legion hall or its clubhouse (a donation in his memory would be appropriate). Also, someone with a house large enough to accommodate all the invitees would provide a warm, homey setting.

The sky is literally the limit if you want to hold the gathering outdoors: a public or private garden, a park, a mountain meadow, or any other meaningful, attractive, and accessible venue. The service for an outdoorsman who particularly loved surf fishing took place on a beach where he made many of his most memorable catches. A teenaged star of her soccer team who died far too soon was remembered on her high school's field, with the audience seated in the stands.

The service itself can include symbolic or ethnic rituals—candles or flower petals or released doves.

EULOGIES

A eulogy is traditional at both funerals and memorial services. As you prepare your remarks or assist others with theirs, consider the following guidelines:

- Create your verbal portrait in an honest and loving way, full of stories that, if you'll pardon the expression, bring the person to life. Don't be afraid to be funny; humor is indeed the best medicine, especially at times of sadness. Above all, be positive. Uncle Fred may have rubbed any number of people the wrong way—possibly you, too—or done things in the course of his life about which neither he nor anyone else was proud, but a funeral or memorial service isn't the place to bring them up. You'll want to avoid what happened to a minister hired by a family to conduct the funeral of someone with whom, had they not been related, they never would have had anything to do. When the minister asked the family members for positive things that he could include in his eulogy, they couldn't come up with a single one. When the service reached the eulogy portion, the minister was reduced to asking the congregation, "And who can tell us something nice about the dearly departed?" After a few minutes of silence that seems like a few hours to the minister, someone in the back row stood and said, "Well, his brother was worse."

- Verify your facts. You don't want your listeners to mutter, "No, Fred and Mary were married in 1968."

- Many cultures try to shield children from death, especially attending funerals. If that is not your tradition, allowing—and indeed, encouraging—a young person to speak about a grandparent, parent, or another loved one is a way for the child to verbalize feelings. One who is old enough to read has the option of preparing remarks in advance or speaking spontaneously. One who can't yet read can be prepared in advance through such questions as, "Remember the time Uncle Fred took you to the zoo?" Or—and these are often the most poignant and memorable—a youngster simply walks up to the pulpit or lectern and speaks spontaneously from the heart.

- Ten minutes is generally long enough, especially when others will speak, too. If there will indeed be others, check among yourselves to avoid duplicating stories. In one unfortunate instance (although it has no doubt happened innumerable times), someone was all set to relate what she considered to be *the* anecdote that epitomized the deceased's life and then, to her great dismay, heard the two preceding speakers tell the exact same story.

- Print out your notes or your entire speech in a type size that you can easily read, and practice reading it out aloud. If you aren't comfortable with public speaking—actors, politicians, clergy, and trial lawyers have an advantage in that regard—rehearse in front of your family or friends until you're completely familiar with what you will say. Your delivery shouldn't sound mechanical, nor should you stare down at the pages. You can pause for effect, and make eye contact with people whom you mention. In short, work at trying to act and sound natural.

Eulogies frequently incorporate poetry, song lyrics, and/or excerpts from fiction or nonfiction books, especially when the material more accurately and more easily conveys the speaker's feelings than one's own words can. By the same token, some people prefer to recite a poem or read from a book or essay instead of composing a eulogy. A good starting place is to look for appropriate literary quotations in *Bartlett's Familiar Quotations* and *The Columbia World of Quotations* (see Appendix F for more ideas).

Music has always been an integral part of funerals, from chanted or sung prayers for the dead to hymns and instrumental processionals and recessionals. Some religions allow only traditional funeral music, but others are open to suggestions—and performances—by family and friends. The member of the clergy who will conduct the service can guide you in that matter.

Memorial services give you greater latitude. If there's an opportunity to choose music, consider songs or melodies that have some connection with the deceased. For example, Uncle Fred's penchant for humming his college's football "fight song" could inspire a church organ arrangement or a recorded version as the service's recessional. So could a melody that everyone would recognize as what Fred and his late wife considered to be "our song."

Perhaps even more poignant, someone told me about a memorial service for a premature baby that included prenatal classical selections that had been played for the child while in the womb.

On a somewhat brighter note, the person whose life was being celebrated at a memorial service at the assisted living facility where she lived was a proud member of the facility's kazoo band. Kazoos were distributed at the end of the service, and everyone—from the person's grandchildren to residents well into their eighties and nineties—played "Amazing Grace."

Like poems and prose, song lyrics can express how mourners feel about the deceased: a gathering to celebrate the life of an inveterate optimist might welcome "Blue Skies" or Louis Armstrong's "What a Wonderful World." The point is that music need not be "classical" or even typically funereal; several funeral directors reported that popular music is often worked into a service, similar to the opening scene of the movie *The Big Chill*, in which an organ arrangement of the Rolling Stones' "You Can't Always Get What You Want" was heard over the opening scene's church funeral.

A friend or relative who sings or plays an instrument can be invited to perform, as can a hired string quartet, jazz band, bluegrass band, or any other small ensemble. Or a guitar player can lead the audience in songs that celebrate the human spirit.

Music is also appropriate at a graveside ceremony; never does a bagpipe sound more mournful than when "Flowers of the Forest" or "Amazing Grace" accompanies the casket being lowered into the ground.

A modern way to mourn and celebrate a life is by means of a memorial website. A cyber-savvy friend or relative or a professional site-builder can build a web page dedicated to the loved one, with a message board on which photos, videos, anecdotes, and other visual and written recollections can be posted. There might be links to the loved one's high school, college, hometown, vacation spots, favorite music, favorite sports teams—anything that's meaningful. A link through which visitors can make a donation to a charity or other beneficial cause in the loved one's name is also appropriate. In addition, if the deceased had a social network page, you can post a notice that notifies "friends" of a person's death, with updates about the funeral/memorial service, notes about other observances, and suggestions for charitable donations. You and others may also want to post recollections there.

MILITARY BURIALS

To be eligible for military honors and benefits, the deceased must have been on active duty or in the Selected Reserve or have served on active duty and left the service under conditions other than dishonorable discharge.

The burial ceremony will include the presentation of an American flag to the next of kin. The flag may first have been draped over the casket and then removed, folded into a triangle, and presented by either the funeral director or a guard of honor (if there is one), or a folded flag may simply be given at the ceremony's conclusion.

The family may request the participation of an honor guard, if one is available, from a nearby military base. Consisting of no fewer than two members of the armed forces, the detail will include at least one member of the branch in which the deceased served. The ceremony may also include a bugler's playing "Taps," if a bugler is available (if not, an electronic recording will be substituted).

There may also be three rifle volleys fired over the casket by an honor guard (again, if available), which should not be confused with a twenty-one-gun salute or indeed any other type of "gun salute." Although the firing detail can consist of any number of personnel, a team of eight is most usual. Each member fires three times, harking back to the days when three shots fired at the end of a truce during a battle signaled that the field had been cleared of its dead. It is traditional that three spent cartridges are folded into the presentation flag.

Families of eligible veterans request such honors through their funeral director, who makes arrangements with the appropriate military service.

Burial benefits available to veterans include a gravesite in any facility that has available space, together with perpetual care, a headstone or marker, a burial flag, and a presidential memorial certificate, all at no cost to the family. Cremated remains are treated in the same manner and with the same honors as casketed remains. Spouses and dependents may be buried with the veteran, again at no cost, and they may be buried there in the event they predecease the veteran.

In certain circumstances, a burial allowance that reimburses the family for funeral expenses is available. The Veterans Benefits Administration will provide details.

The most frequently asked question about military funerals is who may be buried in the prestigious Arlington National Cemetery in Arlington, Virginia, resting place of many presidents and war heroes and site of the Tomb of the Unknown Soldier. Eligibility is more restrictive than in other military cemeteries, but not impossibly so.

CHAPTER 4

Grief Counseling and Therapy

> *"Loss is nothing else but change, and change is Nature's delight."*
>
> **—Marcus Aurelius,** *Meditations*

The grief that follows the death of a loved one is as inevitable and as natural as death itself. You and the other mourners should expect to experience a period of sorrow. How long that period will last is impossible to predict, because not all deaths are alike and not everyone has the same emotional capabilities and responses.

Much will depend on at what age and in what manner the loved one died. Response to someone who died peacefully in his or her nineties might evoke sadness, acceptance, and gratitude for the person's long life. Entirely different reactions—disbelief or denial, anger, and depression—would be expected when a soldier is killed in a military action or a teenager in a car accident, or a child lost to cancer or a baby to Sudden Infant Death Syndrome.

STAGES OF GRIEF

The psychiatrist Elisabeth Kübler-Ross advanced the idea of five stages of grief. Although she applied them with regard to what a dying patient experiences when informed of a life-ending condition, many people say that the progression applies as accurately to the death of a loved one.

The first stage, denial—which can be characterized as "No, it didn't happen! It couldn't have happened!"—is followed by anger, a rage at the realization that the death did in fact occur. That anger can be directed at God or a specific person or just the general situation, but it's a seething or perhaps thunderous fury. The third stage, bargaining—"Let me live another year, and I'll be a better person" applies more to a dying patient than to mourners, but there are survivors who plead, "Take me and bring back my son or daughter."

Then comes a period of depression, during which nothing seems to matter and there may be a loss of appetite, lack of interest in being with old friends, and/or neglecting lifelong hobbies or sports. Finally comes acceptance; the loved one's death is put into its proper perspective and the mourner moves on with life.

Dr. Roberta Temes suggests another behavioral sequence. First comes a feeling of numbness brought on by the realization that someone you love has died. You function, but only mechanically—going through the motions without really wanting to do anything. You're numb, and that numbness doesn't make you want to be in the company of anyone. Then comes a feeling of disorganization when the sense of loss is so great that it interferes with your memory; you put a kettle on the stove but forget to turn on the burner or you forget that you already returned a phone call. Finally comes what Dr. Temes calls "reorganization," when you return to normal behavior.

Although both progressions have their relevance and present useful ways to analyze the mourning process, many health care professionals emphasize that people don't always experience every step or in the order that Drs. Kübler-Ross and Temes suggest.

FORMS OF GRIEF

How people grieve is often determined, if not dictated, by societal forces. Some cultures allow, and indeed encourage, great shows of sorrow: sobbing, hair-tearing, breast-beating, and mourners throwing themselves on coffins and practically into graves. Other cultures take a stoic "stiff upper lip" approach; fans of classic films will remember the scene in *Mrs. Miniver* that portrayed an English family's outwardly restrained reaction to a young person's death during World War II. Similarly, and in real life, John Kelly (who was best known for being the father of Princess Grace of Monaco) included in his will that he wanted no graveside displays of emotion because "Thoroughbreds grieve in the heart."

For whatever reason, mourning in cold-climate cultures tend to be restrained; cultures in warmer climates are likely to be more emotional. The mourning period, too, is marked by cultural variation. For example, Orthodox Jews observe mourning rituals for a year, while widows in some Mediterranean regions wear black dresses for a year, if not the rest of their lives. Although most people do not take bereavement to such lengths (at least outwardly), their sense of loss is no less intense.

A common long-term reaction is a kind of renewed grieving, consciously or subconsciously, as the anniversary of a loved one's death approaches and arrives, no matter how far in the past the death occurred.

The fact that the duration of grief varies as much as its depths gives rise to the issue of "how much is too much?" The answer is the same as how intense should grief be: it depends. The mode of death is a relevant factor. The peaceful departure of an aged relative is relatively easy to accept. That's not to say that a surviving spouse's world will not be radically altered or a son or daughter who looked after the parent won't be similarly affected, but other relatives may find their lives no different from when the person was still alive. However, such tragic deaths as a teenager's suicide may be an event from which relatives and friend may not recover for many years, if indeed they ever recover.

Age and timing can indeed become factors. A woman who lost her sister to a debilitating disease when they were both preadolescents looked back to that time. "I had the choice of thinking about my sister or not," she reflected, meaning that she'd become accustomed to the idea that her sister was dying so she didn't have to dwell on it. She contrasted her reaction to that of an adult relative who more recently lost his brother to a fast-acting brain tumor and could think of nothing but his brother for a very long time.

Psychologists and social workers distinguish between normal and complicated (their word for "excessive") grief behaviors. During the first few months after a loss, many signs and symptoms of normal grief are the same as those of complicated grief.

However, while normal grief symptoms gradually start to fade within six months or so, those of complicated grief get worse or linger for months or even years. Complicated grief manifests itself as being in a chronic, heightened state of mourning and will require attention and action. That is part of your role as overseer: You must become aware that relatives and friends may at some point need professional assistance to come to grips with the loved one's passing.

We're not talking about mourners who become teary-eyed while glancing at a photo of the departed or hearing a song that was "their" song and then going about their business. That's normal grief. Complicated grief is when you drop in at eleven o'clock in the morning to find the bereaved with a glass of vodka in her hand and realizing it wasn't her first of the day. Or having to try to talk someone out of driving to the cemetery in a blizzard because there's "something I have to tell my [late] boy and it can't wait."

Most other behavioral changes may or may not be so dramatic. Among the more common complicated brands of grief are changes in sleep patterns, such as insomnia or spending too much time in bed as a way to escape reality. Changes in eating habits, such as loss of appetite or gorging oneself, is a warning sign, as is a preoccupation with the subject of death—some people pore over the obituary page or can talk about nothing else besides loss of lives. Extreme focus on the loved one and reminders of that person, such as never getting around to removing clothing from a closet, is not what health professionals call normal grief.

Episodes of panic or anxiety or of inexplicable and prolonged anger at the smallest thing can become extreme bitterness over the loss. There can be lack of attention to one's appearance—not changing clothes or combing one's hair or shaving—and to doing such simple household chores as emptying ashtrays or taking out the garbage. Withdrawal from social activities even with close friends or relatives for a prolonged period of time is a problem sign, as is slacking off at work, including prolonged absences. Particularly dangerous is overdependence on prescription drugs (e.g., taking too many tranquillizers) and alcohol and/ or drug abuse.

EXPLAINING DEATH TO YOUNG CHILDREN

Grasping the concept that death is permanent is among the hardest things for a young child to understand, which is why brief, uncomplicated explanations and answers are the most effective. A child can understand health and physical limitations; a good way to explain an elderly person's death, for example, might be to say, "Grandma got sicker and sicker until her body became too sick for it to keep on working."

Using such expressions as "Grandma is at rest," "gone away," or "sleeping, but won't wake up" has very real consequences above and beyond the ease of explaining in such terms. You don't want children to think that anyone—including themselves—who is resting or sleeping will never wake up or that a person who is away on vacation or a business trip will never return. If the child's family religion subscribes to an afterlife, consult with a member of the clergy about ways to present that concept.

A child whose pet has died will have experienced loss, and this can be a good reference point in any discussion of a human death. It's particularly helpful to reassure a child that feeling sad is perfectly natural: "People cry when they feel sad, which is why everyone is crying about Grandma."

Whether a child should attend a funeral depends on the youngster's age and emotional capacity to handle the situation. Some may take viewing the body in stride, while others may find it too much.

"Will you die, Mommy?" and "Will I die, Daddy?" are inevitable questions. Psychologists and social workers applaud parents who respond with a simple, "Oh, not for a very long time, so there's no reason even to think about it now."

Some youngsters, especially teenagers, direct a great deal of anger toward their parents because they perceive the parents as forcing them to mourn whether or not they wanted to at any given time. They also feel a kind of jealousy toward the deceased, especially if it happens to have been a sibling, for taking away their parents' attention. As a young woman reflected, "I knew my parents wanted me to grieve, and somehow I started to resent them. Every other kid's mother was pretty proud of the fact that they were learning to ice-skate; with my mother, it was pretty halfhearted. . . . The anger at my parents subsided as soon as they stopped trying to get me to talk about it and let me get on with my life. At that point, I stopped being angry at the situation. My mother became interested in what I was doing and started dealing with me and her. We started getting together, and that was good."

Since young children and adolescents tend to be unwilling or unable to articulate their unhappiness, they display it instead through their behavior. Warning signs include depression and even moodiness above and beyond "normal" teenage angst. An example of such behavior would be a preoccupation with death, especially talk of suicide, which might take the form of talk of a reunion with the deceased. On the other hand, an inability to talk about the deceased is equally problematic. As with adults, prolonged withdrawal from social activities shows complicated grief. So do school truancy and a radical change in the youngster's type of friends, such as going from being a part of an upbeat, clean-cut crowd to hanging around with a group of goths, with accompanying changes in hairstyle and wardrobe. More glaring still would be running away from home and alcohol and/or drug abuse, which must be interpreted as loud cries for help.

Feelings of guilt that can overwhelm both adults and youngsters come from a real or imagined sense of shirked responsibility. Examples are numerous as people try to make sense of senseless situations. "If only I hadn't bought her that car for her birthday," sobs a heartbroken father after his teenaged daughter was killed by an oncoming vehicle. "If only they had left the party ten minutes later, or if only I had come to get her" echoes the parents of a youngster whom the driver had given a lift home. "I should have insisted that he see the doctor a year ago," says a widow, "because maybe then we could have caught the cancer in time." "If only I had done better in school, Grandpa would still be with us," adds her granddaughter.

More devastating is the reaction of someone who bears some responsibility: the negligent driver who survives an auto accident in which a passenger is killed, or the friend who doesn't insist "hard enough" that a friend who has had too much to drink should hand over the car keys.

No matter how hard you and others try to make the guilt-racked person "see reason," you can't unless and until the person works through the feeling. All you as a layperson can do is provide support by being there in person or spirit. Someone who lost a child at a young age recalls how a friend would come every day for a year just to sit across from the mother and be there as she cried. Conversation was not necessary, but the friend's presence was.

However, at precisely the time when a network of comforting friends and relations is most welcome, mourners may find that they are shunned. When his wife died, a husband found that people he considered good friends and neighbors at the senior residence where he and his wife lived all but ostracized him, as if his wife's death could rub off on them (that's not an uncommon reaction, a psychologist confirmed, especially among older people). Similarly, but for other reasons, male friends and neighbors of a forty-something man who lost his wife resented him because of the attention that their wives were paying him; the men all but acknowledged that the casseroles the women brought and the other help they gave the widower could lead to another kind of comforting. Nevertheless, the isolation the man felt added to his pain.

Physicians point to another complicated grief indication that should be looked out for: a change in the physical condition of a surviving spouse, especially an older person and especially if the loved one succumbed to a long-term disease or condition. It is as though the survivor stayed alive for her spouse's sake; now that the husband has died, the widow "allows" herself to reveal her own medical problems. Those problems often become severe to the point of life threatening, since the stress of the loss is likely to accelerate or exacerbate the illness. Therefore, persuading a surviving spouse to have a medical check-up is a good idea. It's also wise for any mourner who "isn't feeling quite right" physically as well as emotionally.

COUNSELING VS. THERAPY

Professional attention is available in the forms of grief counseling and grief therapy to help mourners through the rough times. "Counseling" applies to the process of working through normal grief to a healthy and satisfying conclusion within a reasonable time. "Therapy" uses specialized techniques designed to assist people with complicated grief reactions resolve the problems, especially where one or more other psychological or psychosomatic issues are involved. They should be considered opportunities to help restore a new "normality" by coming to grips with loss and developing a new and workable relationship with the loved one.

The therapist's goal is to help mourners with all the feelings they have in relation to their loss—not only the actual loss, but also losses of self that mourners can feel. For example, a mourner may experience a feeling of relief at and after the death of a relative with whom she had an ambivalent relationship, a reaction coming from the realization that she never again must deal with whatever it was that bothered her about the person. If that creates feelings of guilt, the therapist can help the person understand and accept them in the safe, nonjudgmental environment of the therapist's office.

Therapy is an equally valuable tool in the process of identifying and coping with feelings of dependency. A widow who had been told by her husband that she had no "head for finances" suddenly found herself faced with daunting tasks of paying bills and reconciling bank statements, chores that her husband had handled. However, once she found that she was perfectly capable of writing checks and balancing checkbooks, her fear turned to anger at her husband for having considered her such a helpless "hothouse flower."

Dealing with finances can be a troubling issue in another way. The surviving spouse of a two-income household may have to learn to live with reduced resources, with the prospects of not having enough money to last for the rest of one's life a frightening reality. Again, therapy can help the person face and accept such fears, as well as finding ways to deal with the prospect (therapists have networks of their own, which can include financial planners).

There's no stigma involved in taking advantage of grief counseling and therapy. Grief counselors are routinely called in after traumatic events: 9/11, the Columbine High School and Virginia Tech massacres, plane crashes, mine cave-ins, and similar disasters. They help not only survivors and families of those who perished but also anyone else in the community who needs assistance.

Psychologists and social workers, some of whom specialize as "grief counselors," offer individual and group sessions. Members of the clergy, whether or not they are affiliated with a house of worship, are usually trained to offer support. Hospitals and hospices have programs. City, county, and state social service agencies are yet another source, and funeral homes often offer aftercare programs. Crisis intervention hotlines provide referrals. Within the broad category of grief counseling and therapy are group programs aimed at people in specific situations, including surviving spouses and families of cancer victims, crime victims, or people who have committed suicide.

Counselors and therapists have their own techniques based on an assessment of the mourner's needs. The approaches might involve keeping a journal or other forms of creative writing, meditation, the use of possessions that belonged to the deceased, role-playing, and art and music therapy. The widely used "empty chair technique" has the mourner address an empty chair as if the deceased were in it followed by the mourner's sitting in the chair and playing the role of the deceased. Some modes of counseling and therapy request or require the participation of other people, such as the mourner's family and/or close friends. This is the nature of support.

REFLECTIONS OF A SURVIVING SPOUSE

"When my husband killed himself—which was a shock but not a surprise, since he was clinically depressed and on medication—I went through each and every 'classic' phase of grief. It was as if the manual had been written about me: shock, grief, denial, numbness, anger, sadness, and finally acceptance.

"At the time I wondered if I could ever get through a day (or night) without crying. Eventually, three or four months later, I did just that. Then, I wondered if I'd ever get through a day (or night) without thinking of John. Eventually, three or four years later, I did just that. Finally, now twelve years out and counting, I go days and weeks without thinking of John, but there are always triggers that recall a memory—seeing a raccoon (a special animal for us), hearing a pileated woodpecker, smelling a particular brand of leather cleaner, or using our wedding china. I still think of John often, but now it is without rancor and instead with a twisted grin of bittersweet memory.

"I got standard counseling from my rector (the one who married us and the one who buried John). Nothing more, though.

"What brought me solace was the fact that I *had* to continue working, both my own work and John's. He was a steeplechase trainer, and had several horses in training. I took over for him when he died. Funny thing, the old saw in the horse business is that 'nobody ever committed suicide that has a fast two-year-old in the barn!' Curiously, John did just that. The 'fast two-year-old' turned out to be a dual champion steeplechaser (over hurdles, then over timber) and is still foxhunting today. I see the horse sometimes and think—how would this be surprising?—of my poor, sweet husband.

"The hardest part was the yawning chasm of loneliness that grasps you with icy fingers the first night … week … month that you are alone. At first, all your friends and family surround you, hold you tight, nurture you. They stay for a bit, but then, one by one, they go back to their own lives. Eventually, you're alone. That is unsettling. I was lucky to have the horses to lean on. I dried many, many tears in the manes of my horses.

"I coped the same way anyone else copes with tragedy—by muddling through. Did I do okay? I'd say so. I'm out the other side.

"If I could change anything, it would be that my last words to John would not have been in annoyance (a horsemanship argument—nothing important but terse) but instead in love. This made me into a far more gentle, more kind person. I think it has to. I think of that horrible, black, bleak feeling I had for a few weeks after John's death—a sort of mini-depression. And I grieve—my heart aches—that, as a person suffering from depression, John and others like him feel that way *every single day.* What a horrifying thought."

A self-help therapy in which grievers can take part on their own is by helping others. Go to a child's or grandchild's baseball or soccer game or swim meet; your presence and support will be appreciated. Take a grandchild or a niece or nephew or a young neighbor on a "shopping spree"—the purchases needn't be expensive, but the shared experience will give immediate pleasure and create wonderful memories for everyone. Get involved in a church or community group, or volunteer at a pet rescue organization. Motivating yourself or another mourner may not be easy, but once you're out and involved, you'll find that you've reconnected with life.

Perhaps the best reflection on how people cope with death and the grieving process comes from Rabbi Eric Eisenkramer:

> A rabbi friend, David Whiman, told me about the funeral of a man who was survived by his wife, a woman who was ninety-two years old. The day of the funeral it was snowing and cold and all of the mourners gathered around the graveside for the service. The rabbi began and after a few moments, the family realized that the widow was gone. They turned around to discover that she was walking away from the graveside as fast as she could, trudging through the snow. The mourners looked at each other for a moment in shock, and then went after her.
>
> "Within a few minutes the widow was brought back to the graveside. She called the rabbi over. He leaned down to listen, hoping to help her deal with her obvious grief. And the woman said, 'Rabbi, it's cold, make it quick.'
>
> "Truly, we all deal with grief in our own ways."

CHAPTER 5

Housekeeping

> *"Organization can never be a substitute for initiative and for judgment."*
>
> **—Justice Louis D. Brandeis**

Sometime after and sometime before the funeral comes a procession of procedures that can best be lumped together as "housekeeping." The time line is affected by how soon the funeral is after the time of death. If the funeral is to be held within a day or two, "housekeeping" will perforce begin afterward; if longer, some of the chores can happen before the funeral.

These are administrative chores that range from wrapping up aspects of the loved one's daily life to gathering documents and other information in anticipation of probating the loved one's estate and handling other legal and financial matters.

You'll need copies of the death certificate for many purposes. The funeral director, who by now has filed the completed document with the county bureau of records, will routinely arrange to get copies for you: you'll want twelve to fifteen of them. A copy costs anywhere from $10 to $15, although some counties charge less per copy when they are bought in quantity. A certified copy will be required for money-related matters, such as for probate and when dealing with banks and insurance companies. Otherwise, a photocopy will suffice, and you can always copy one from a certified copy.

You can obtain extra copies without going through the funeral home. Do so in person at the county clerk's office or via the Web. If the latter, use a search engine under "death certificates" and the county name and state.

According to law, the post office will hold the person's mail for fifteen days after learning of his or her death, after which the mail will be returned to the sender. Therefore, file a change of address form, which will require showing the postmaster a letter of authority such as a note from the probate court, although a family member can show proper identification and a copy of the death certificate.

You've already stopped newspaper home delivery for someone who lived alone. Now cancel the cable television, Internet provider, cell phone service, and other monthly charges, giving priority to those payments that are automatically charged to a credit card or deducted from a bank account.

If the deceased had lived alone in a house that he or she owned, you might want to continue to use the services of a gardener and a pest control company and, if there's a swimming pool, a pool cleaning service so the property looks its sparkling best when it's shown to prospective buyers or when it is taken over by its new owner.

The representative of any person who had been receiving Social Security benefits should telephone the Social Security Administration (SSA) as soon after the death as practicable (the toll-free number is 1-800-772-1213). If monthly benefits were being paid via direct deposit, notify the bank or other financial institution of the death, and request that any funds received for the month of death and later be returned to Social Security as soon as possible. If benefits were being paid by check, do not cash or deposit it. That's because any payment made during the month of the death must be refunded, even if the payment were deposited on the third of the month and the deceased died on the twenty-eighth. That sounds unfair, but the law is the law.

It is also a good idea to get in touch with the SSA promptly is to reduce the chance of identity theft or fraud using the Social Security number.

Another reason to be in touch with Social Security is to determine whether death and survivor benefits are due. A onetime benefit of $265 (at this time) for burial expenses is available, for which either a surviving spouse (or child entitled to survivor benefits) or the funeral director can complete the application and apply the benefit directly to the funeral bill.

COLLECTING INFORMATION AND DOCUMENTATION

Now comes the real test of your sense of organization: collecting information and documentation. Although you notified the deceased's place of business at the time of death, find out from the company's human resources department (if the company is large enough to have one) or anyone else knowledgeable about such matters as any unpaid salary and/or commissions, compensation for unused sick or vacation time; life insurance, retirement plan, or pension; and death benefits, including funeral and/or burial assistance. You'll also want to know about health coverage for surviving family members, and specifically which benefits are transferable and at what rate.

As you plow through papers and come across a life insurance policy, find out from the agent with whom the deceased dealt or the company itself about how to expedite payment to the policy's beneficiary. Find out, too, what the status of the policy is; perhaps it had been borrowed against and there's an outstanding loan. In many instances, a letter, a bill, or checkbook entry is evidence that a policy exists, but you still can't find it no matter how many times you turn the house upside down. In that case, you must learn the procedure of filing a claim without having the policy at hand.

Checkbooks and credit card statements are fertile sources for clues about other financial matters, too. A payment to a mortgage company or an auto insurance agency will lead you to people there who'll provide you with relevant information: in these instances, how close the house is to being paid up, and how much the estate may be entitled to from a refund when the car is sold. In addition, keep an eye out for any or all of the following if relevant: birth certificate (for the deceased and the immediate family); adoption records; marriage documents (license, prenuptial agreement, divorce decree, child custody papers); military service record (especially discharge papers); real estate deed or lease; business ownership or partnership agreements; immigration and/or citizenship papers; and vehicle registration (car, truck, motorcycle, boat, airplane).

You'll also want to check with the deceased's investment counselor about a securities portfolio, and with the accountant about tax returns. The name of the game is to compile as complete a file about all aspects of the loved one's life as you can collect.

Two other postfuneral matters cannot be considered mere "housekeeping" chores: buying and unveiling a headstone; and going through and disposing of the loved one's personal effects.

HEADSTONES

If your loved one's remains were buried, a memorial headstone (they're no longer referred to as "tombstones") to mark the grave is customarily erected or "unveiled" any time within the first year. Granite or bronze are the most durable materials from which headstones are made, and so they are the most frequently used.

Although stones come in a wide range of sizes and colors, your selection may be limited to cemetery regulations. Many cemeteries have strict restrictions, so ask questions before you commit to buying a stone:

- Are there any restrictions on the material from which the stone is made? Are there any color restrictions?
- Are there minimum and/or maximum dimensions? That can be an issue when the memorial is more than one person, such as spouses or significant others. Would a carved projection, such as an angel, be calculated into the overall size?
- What are the permissible shapes: upright? flat and raised off the ground? flat and flush to the ground?
- Can a floral vase be included as part of the stone?
- Are there any other requirements or restrictions? Some cemeteries insist on lawn mower–proof

edges for granite bases. Cemeteries affiliated with a church or a faith may require a religious symbol to be incorporated into the memorial design.

- What permit or authorization is required before a stone is installed?
- What are the delivery and installation procedures for the memorial headstone, and what if any fees apply?

Headstones are available from monument companies, many if not most of which are located near one or more cemeteries. These companies create the memorial by sandblasting names and designs into the stone or etching them onto the bronze, then arrange for transportation and installation. An advantage is that these companies have showrooms or can otherwise display selections. Other sources include the cemetery itself, funeral directors, casket retail stores, and Internet monument dealers. All in this grouping usually outsource the actual work, so prices tend to reflect their commissions.

- No matter from whom you order the stone, be sure you're satisfied with regard to the lettering's depth and finish and, if there is a design, all its elements and proportions. (This is especially important when room must be left for the name and dates of a surviving spouse or significant other to be added later.) Also be aware that since granite is a quarried stone, minor imperfections are inevitable.

- Bronze grave markers are cast from bronze poured into a mold. The raised portions of the design and lettering are typically polished to highlight the bronze color.

- A marker's lettering and raised relief should have adequate definition, and the paint and clear-coat finish should be evenly applied.

- As for the cost, prices vary widely—and often wildly—depending on the material and any decoration (such as a vase or a ceramic portrait on the stone). Additional lettering for an epitaph is another expense. Competition among vendors is still another factor. As ever, the best advice is to take your time and shop around.

DISPOSING OF THE LOVED ONE'S PERSONAL EFFECTS

Facing anyone who has suffered the loss of a loved one is the need to dispose of that person's personal effects. In this context "personal effects" means more than just hairbrush or cufflinks; the phrase can encompass one or more pets, furniture, and other household items, sporting equipment, car, a boat—in short, any possession.

The task's difficulty comes from emotional attachments: memories of the loved one's attachment to the article, one or more survivors' attachment to it, and—hardest of all—the link between the loved one and the survivors that the item represents.

When and how this disbursal will take place may depend on time constraints, such as vacating rented premises for which a new tenant (and a demanding landlord) is waiting or tax considerations. There are likely to be emotional factors, too: Disposing of personal effects is a stark physical confirmation that the loved one is gone, often just as stark as watching the casket being lowered into the ground or seeing the ashes placed in a crypt or being scattered in the wind or water. As such, many people are reluctant to "let go," and they delay the "cleaning out and getting rid" process as long as possible. A closet full of clothing can be an unconscious wish that the loved one will return to wear them; some mourners even insist on keeping the loved one's room and all its furnishings intact, as if a shrine to the departed.

Psychologists and social workers, as well as people who have mourned, agree that, whether or not with help from others, even the most reluctant among us will eventually address and act on the matter. Just as mourning takes as long as it takes, so too will this part of the grieving process. Those who recently lost a loved one may not accept that reality, and indeed no one ever stops missing or loving that person, but there does come a time when you'll hear yourself say, "I'm ready . . . let's do it."

A poignant example of admitting that a loved one has gone and that life must move on can be seen in the movie *The Americanization of Emily*, when Emily's mother, a World War II widow, finally comes to grips with the combat loss of both her husband and son.

In many instances, your loved one has made disposing of the possessions easier by making specific bequests in his or her Will. These wishes must be honored, before or while the Will is being probated. As an example of how a Will facilitates such matters, my mother left a family heirloom grandfather clock to an older nephew who identified the clock with our grand-mother's house in which it held a place of parlor prominence while he was growing up. Another nephew, a younger man who had admired the clock in my parents' house, approached me as my mother's sole heir and her estate's Executor, to ask for the clock if I didn't want it. "The matter is out of my hands," I happily admitted, delighted not to be caught between competing cousins.

Although they don't have the legal force of a Will's specific bequests, gifts indicated in a letter from the loved one "to be opened at my death" (or in any correspondence or memorandum, for that matter) should be similarly distributed to the designated recipients.

As for unspecified items, the estate's representative has the final say as to whom they go. Sure, bad blood can come from two or more people wanting the same article, but even if you can't work out a compromise or exhibit the wisdom of a Solomon and threaten to cut the baby grand piano in half, you can still do your best to avoid bloodshed.

Some relatives or friends may express interest in a painting or a clock or another object that may have sentimental value, but then say, "No, on second thought I won't have room for it." In that case, suggest taking a photo of the object as a reminder.

There will, of course, be many things in closets, cupboards, breakfronts, basements, and garages that no one wants. Use creativity to find new homes for objects not worth consigning to the trash. If the deceased was the only person in the family who played golf and none of his usual foursome wants his set of clubs, a local high school or college may have a golf team, or the pro at the club where your loved one played may run a program for youngsters who'd be happy to use them. Both public and school libraries and hospitals and senior-citizen residences are likely recipients of books and music tapes and CDs, and they'll often send someone to pick up the items. The same applies to collections: World War II memorabilia might well be welcomed by an American Legion or Veterans of Foreign Wars chapter or a college history department. Old paintings and photographs may be of interest to a museum or historical society. The youngster who cut the lawn might be delighted to have first crack at anything or everything on the tool bench or hanging in the garage.

Give contemporaries of a young loved one the opportunity to select one or more items by which to remember their friend; they'll also have useful ideas about where their friend's unwanted possessions will do the most good.

If not, there's always eBay (www.ebay.com).

In a similar vein, any number of civic or religious charitable organizations will pick up clothing in good condition—"gently used" is the current euphemism—and then sell the clothes in fund-raising rummage sales or give them to victims of natural disasters and others in need both in this country and abroad. Bric-a-brac, artwork, furniture, and cutlery and other kitchenware are equally welcomed for resale. Ask a member of the clergy or check the photo book or a search engine under "Charities." Be sure to ask for a receipt for the fair market value that the estate can use for tax purposes.

Finally, there are private individuals and firms that purchase estates. The real estate agent who sold my parents' house arranged with one to haul away everything that no one else wanted, and the estate ended up with "found" money.

And speaking of money, the services of an expert assessor would be money well spent (and paid for by the estate) in the event a stamp collection or that old oil painting that only the deceased liked turned out to be valuable.

CHAPTER 6

Probate: An Overview

> *"Let's choose Executors and talk of wills."*
>
> **—Shakespeare,** *King Richard the Second*

L et's begin with a few legal terms that we'll encounter in the next few chapters, starting with "probate," the process that authorizes property in the decedent's estate to go to his or her beneficiaries. The "decedent" is just what it sounds like—the deceased person; "estate" means all the assets and debts the decedent had at the time of death.

Most probate work involves a Will, a document signed by the Will-maker, or testator, indicating where the property is to go.

The person designated in a Will to administer the estate is the Executor (a female Executor is properly, but not always, referred to as an Executrix). In some states, that person is called the Personal Representative, but for our purposes, we'll use the word "Executor."

Anyone of legal age can qualify as an Executor: unless the assignment goes to the testator's lawyer, it typically goes to a spouse, a son or daughter, another relative, or a friend. Being an Executor is a paying job; the fee is based on the value of the estate, although many Executors who are relatives or close friends will forgo any compensation. Some Wills designate co-Executors, with one being a bank or another financial institution if the estate is substantial or complicated. If a person named as Executor has died or otherwise can't serve, the court will appoint a substitute.

Shortly after the testator's death, the Executor files certain papers in the probate court (called in some states, the surrogate court) in the county where the testator lived.[1] The Executor demonstrates to the court's satisfaction that the Will was executed according to applicable formalities; for example, that the number of people who were supposed to witness the document did so. The Executor then gives the court a list of all the estate's property, together with a list of any outstanding debts and the names of the people whom the testator wanted to receive property (they're called the "legatees"). Then the legatees and any creditors are notified that probate has started so they have a chance to contest the

---

[1] We're talking about The Law, which always involves exceptions and local and state variations, but we'll describe customary procedures here.

Will if they wish. The court will have by then issued Letters Testamentary, which confirms that the Executor can act on behalf of the estate.

The majority of Wills are printed; that is, produced on paper by a word-processing computer (typing in the blanks in preprinted forms is so twentieth century), duly signed, and witnessed. Contrary to popular thought, just because a Will is notarized doesn't necessarily mean it complies with all the essential statutory requirements. There are, however, two other types of Wills. A holographic Will is in the testator's handwriting. Such Wills are valid in most states, but there must be some evidence that the testator in fact wrote it, a fact that can be proved by witnesses, handwriting experts, or other methods. Holographic Wills are often created in emergency situations, such as the actual or perceived threat of impending death; even states that don't regularly recognize holographic Wills have declared them valid if an emergency existed. Some thirty states do not require that they be witnessed.

An oral Will, known to lawyers as a nuncupative Will, is spoken, not written. Not many states recognize them except in emergency situations—during war or danger of imminent death—because of the chance of fraud or ambiguity. What constitutes such an emergency differs in the twenty states that allow oral Wills, and in some of those states at least two witnesses must have been present and can swear that testator meant to make a Will.

Dying without having left a Will is called dying "intestate," pronounced "in-TESS-tate" and meaning that the property will be distributed according to the laws of the state in which the decedent lived. That doesn't always jibe with what the decedent might have had in mind. For example, although most people assume that a surviving spouse inherits everything, many states say that the spouse inherits only half the estate, with the remainder going to the intestate's children and other relatives. Stepchildren and nonmarried partners do not inherit under most states' laws of intestacy, while the property of a person who dies leaving no heirs goes to the state. Because a Will-less estate must still go through probate, the court appoints an Administrator (a female is an Administrix) who handles the details for a fee based on the size of the estate.

The above surveys the usual situation, but there are exceptions. Probate may not be required if an estate is worth less than a certain amount. The amount varies from state to state; for example, California law requires probate for any estate worth more then $100,000.

"Summary probate" or "simplified small estate" proceedings are also available. The requirement in New York State is an estate, excluding real estate and amounts set aside for surviving family members, that has a gross value of up to $20,000. Florida law requires an estate of not more than $75,000 or one that has no real estate and assets of any value that are free from creditors' claims except for funeral and certain medical expenses. If so, the courts will authorize property transfer based on only affidavits. But more about that later.

In the event that real estate is located in another state other than where the decedent resided, an ancillary probate will be required before that property can be included in the decedent's estate.

The involvement of a second state raises the question of "residence," an important issue, because residence determines which probate laws will apply. Let's suppose that the deceased lived in Chicago, but had a little lake house in Wisconsin where he went every weekend and vacation. After his retirement, he spent more and more time at the lake, so much so that people used to joke that he "visited" Chicago. Which law then applies: Illinois or Wisconsin? The answer is based on the decedent's intention: the state where he voted, where his driver's license was issued, where he filed state tax returns, where the Will was made, and any other evidence that the person considered himself a resident of one state or the other would be relevant. Some states make the answer easy: Florida requires its residents to live there for six months and a day out of the year . . . and be required to produce proof should the residency be challenged.

YOUR ROLE AS EXECUTOR

Let's say that at some point in your loved one's life—we'll use Uncle Fred as an example again—he asked whether you would serve as Executor when the time came. Before you agree, you asked a lawyer—his, yours, or somebody else's—what would be involved. The lawyer answered your question with questions of his or her own:

- Will you have the available time, or would your business, family obligations, or other commitments interfere? Even the simplest estate requires a commitment, even with a lawyer's assistance, and time schedules set by the probate court must be adhered to.

- How good are you at handling paperwork and legal issues? A sense of organization is essential. Someone who throws bills and receipts into any old shoebox and waits for a second notice isn't exactly Executor material.

- How well do you know the person whose Will you'll administer? You don't have to be the person's best friend in the world, but there may be situations where you'll have to put yourself in his shoes or try to read his mind to carry out the estate's best interests. How qualified and comfortable will you feel doing so?

- How well do you get along with the family? It's a matter that we've encountered earlier, but it bears repeating, because as the old line goes, "Where's there's a Will, there's a relative." Whether or not you're a part of the family, you'll be under scrutiny. You may have to make decisions with which one or more relatives will disagree, and there may be rivalries and jealousies that you'll have to mediate even if one of the parties is your spouse or parent. In other words, how willing are you to risk upsetting domestic tranquility?

• Executors are paid for their work. Many friends and relatives serve without compensation, for the love of and to honor the testator's memory. Although passing up the fee (which comes out of the estate) is not obligatory, it's a factor. Will you be willing to do so?

You answered these questions to your own, Uncle Fred's, and his lawyer's satisfaction, so you were written into the Will as Executor. Now that your time has come, so to speak, you have more questions:

• When does probate begin? Most states have no time limit, but others have a three- or four-year limit. As a practical matter, since most families want to have the estate settled as quickly as possible, Executors are likely to start the proceeding within a month or two. Although a state may require that whoever has possession of a will must submit it to the court within a month after the testator's death, that doesn't count as starting the probate process.

- How long does probate take? Barring the unforeseen, an uncomplicated estate should take no more than six months, and it often takes less. Among factors that affect the time are the nature of the assets (a business may have to be sold, or there may be property in several states); whether a house or coop or condo must be sold; whether there are any tax issues (federal estate tax requirements can take at minimum the better part of a year); and whether beneficiaries contest the will or even just fight over who gets what.

- What does probate cost? That too is difficult to predict. A lawyer who helps the Executor must be paid; so must an appraiser, and an accountant if they are used. Court filing fees for paperwork will be a flat fee or a percentage of the value of the estate's assets, all depending on state law. The current rule of thumb is that an uncomplicated and uncontested estate in which the Executor takes no fee runs roughly 5 percent of the estate's value, but often less. Complex estates will necessarily require more work, as will such complicated situations where custody of minor children becomes an issue.

At some point in your Executorship, you may come across reference to the Uniform Probate Code. In an effort to standardize diverse and diverging state laws in a variety of areas, national conferences of lawyers codified a number of fields. Many, but not necessarily all, states have adopted these codes, one of which deals with probate. Therefore, if the deceased had property in more than one state and all of those states have adopted the UPC, there won't be a conflict . . . maybe (remember: because this is The Law, there are exceptions).

The following states have adopted the UPC in its entirety with, however, significant modifications in some places: Alaska, Arizona, Colorado, Florida, Hawaii, Idaho, Michigan, Minnesota, Montana, Nebraska, New Mexico, North Dakota, South Carolina, South Dakota, and Utah. In addition, many states have adopted parts of the UPC.

There's a growing tendency to simplify the probate process through estate planning that removes the element of transferring assets under a Will. Indeed, probate in many instances can be avoided, a technique that we'll encounter later in this book.

CHAPTER 7

The Probate Process

> *"There is a strange charm in the hope of a good legacy that wonderfully reduces the sorrow people otherwise may feel for the death of their relatives and friends."*
>
> **—Miguel de Cervantes**

We've already mentioned the necessity of locating the loved one's assets and liabilities, but now gathering and inventorying them in a comprehensive and functional fashion (lawyers call it "marshalling") is imperative. That's because the net amount of what the deceased's estate will determine the type, speed, and expense of the probate process.

Even if you did so at the time of his death, now's the time to go through his possessions again, and with an even-finer-tooth comb. Search through bankbooks, checkbooks, and bank statements. Look for statements and correspondence from stockbrokers, mutual funds, and anything else that smacks of investing. Correspondence with insurance companies is important, as are letters to and from state, local, and federal governments that may be evidence of tax liens, refunds, Social Security issues, and any number of other resolved or unresolved financial issues. Tax returns are yet another fertile source of evidence. Search online for unclaimed property, admittedly a long shot, but see what, if anything, comes up when you enter the deceased's full name and Social Security number into Google, Bing, or another search engine.

Leave no stone unturned. Go through his wallet, dresser drawers, top shelves of closets, coat and pants pockets, and cookie jars. Everyone has a secret hiding place, and even if Fred didn't literally hide valuables under his mattress, there's no telling what piece of jewelry or bank passbook may turn up where least expected. Case in point: the grown children of an elderly woman knew that she banked at a certain branch where her Social Security checks were directly deposited, but to their amazement, going through their mother's "unmentionables" drawer after her death unearthed a manila envelope on which was written in their mother's distinctive scrawl "for an emergency." In it were $5,000 in cash and a savings account passbook from another bank that showed ten times that amount. The children's reaction, "Who knew?" should be the mantra of all next of kin and Executors.

Safe-deposit boxes present a special problem. Banks are reluctant to let even people who have possession of the key sift through the box's contents. Therefore, unless someone who is a cosigner can gain access, you'll have to get court authorization and show a copy of the death certificate before you can even look for the Will.

Once you have inventoried the assets, you can determine their value with regard to whether they exceed the monetary maximum for a summary/small estate probate. Not all assets are subject to probate, however: property that is held jointly (the title to which automatically passes to the other person), insurance proceeds to named beneficiaries, and assets held in trust are among those items that are excluded.

Some estates are easy to calculate: a rented apartment or a very small house in a modest neighborhood, an old car, Social Security, a small investment portfolio and savings, and no valuable possessions or fortunes found under the mattress. Others are equally easy, but on the other side of the coin: a house worth millions, an Old Master painting, a thriving business. But unless you know for certain that an estate qualifies for a small estate probate, the services of such professionals as appraisers and real estate brokers will be necessary.

BEGINNING THE PROBATE PROCEDURE

Probate begins with the filing of a petition. The document, which you can get from the probate/surrogate court or download from the Web, calls for such information as the decedent's full name, date of death, and names of survivors and beneficiaries.

A copy of the Will must be attached to the petition. That's not a problem in the majority of instances, but there's always a possibility that the testator executed a later Will. There's also the possibility of one or more "codicils," the word for amendments that changes specific terms in Wills. An example would be naming a new recipient of, say, a painting after the death of the person whom the Will originally left it. Codicils were once prevalent when Wills were handwritten; it was easier to add a separate amendment than to have a scribe or clerk rewrite the entire document. Now, however, they're rare, since all it takes is a couple of keystrokes and out pops an entirely new Will. Nevertheless, codicils still exist, so you should be aware that there might be one.

The next step in the process is to notify all the parties who may have an actual or even a potential interest in the Will that there will be a hearing. Formal notices are sent by mail— "return receipt requested," to be safe—to the beneficiaries who are mentioned in the Will, to people who would stand to inherit if there were no Will (meaning, if the Will should be declared invalid), and to known creditors. With regard to the last group, there's no need to make an exhaustive search, but if you know that the deceased has a mortgage on his house, the bank that holds the mortgage should be notified.

In addition, most states require that a notice run in a local newspaper, customarily in the "legal notices" section. The purpose is, of course, to give any creditors or other interested parties who hadn't been notified by mail the opportunity to participate in the probate hearing. How long the notice must be published varies from jurisdiction to jurisdiction.

Some creditors may choose to file their claims through the probate process. That's up to them, but those who don't will lose their right to collect after a certain period of time.

The hearing customarily takes place several weeks after the petition is filed. Although it's usually a formality, to the extent that few of the people notified bother to appear, there can be very real problems. For example, there can be a question about whether the testator's signature on the Will is valid; statements from witnesses to the Will can resolve that issue. Or one beneficiary can allege that another exerted undue influence over the testator in order to receive a larger piece of the pie. That's almost always a complicated question, and one that will require the judge to hear evidence and then make a ruling.

But if there are no objections, the court will approve the petition and issue Letters Testamentary to the Executor or personal representative.

Whenever someone dies intestate or when the person named as Executor is unable or unwilling to serve (for example, the named Executor predeceases the testator and a new Executor wasn't designated before the testator died), the court will appoint an Administrator to handle the process. That's usually a close relative (but not a minor child) or a person who will inherit some portion of the estate, although the family lawyer or a court-appointed designee might be selected. This Administrator serves as the functional equivalent of an Executor.

If the Will doesn't explicitly stipulate that the Executor is to serve without posting a bond, the judge may require one. Such a bond, which certain insurance companies issue, protects the estate in the event the Executor's actions cause the estate to lose money. Even if the Will is silent on the matter, all the beneficiaries can agree that the Executor needn't post a bond, although the judge has discretion to insist that one be posted. Probate bonds cannot be canceled before the closing of the estate except by court order. The Executor or administrator is personally responsible for paying the premiums until his or her liability under the bond is terminated, even if there are no funds left in the estate. If a bond is indeed required, someone familiar with the probate process can suggest where to apply for one.

OPENING AN ESTATE ACCOUNT AND DIVIDING THE ESTATE

Once you receive your authorizing Letters Testamentary, you're ready to start your job in earnest. First, open a bank account in the name of the estate using funds that you will transfer from the deceased's personal account(s). But before you can do so, you must obtain from the Internal Revenue Service a Tax ID number for yourself as the estate's Executor or Administrator (see Appendix H).

Once you've opened an account in the estate's name, do not use your own money from this point; commingling funds is troublesome and in some cases illegal. However, you or anyone else are entitled to be reimbursed for any cash previously laid out, such as paying for the funeral flowers or for repairs to the deceased's car before you try to sell it.

Use the estate account to take care of obvious debts, such as final medical bills and funeral expenses, the monthly mortgage payment, and taxes . . . especially taxes.

You may be sure that as soon as you are officially named Executor, the Will's named beneficiaries will ask when they can get what's coming to them. The short answer is, all in good time.

DISTRIBUTING THE ASSETS

Some things can be distributed right away: the painting to the daughter designated in the Will or the grandfather clock to the nephew similarly named. As for monetary gifts, whether cash or securities, you must be certain that the estate will have enough to cover taxes, which are priority number one.

Items that aren't mentioned usually pass under a Will's residual clause, which could call for anything from a roughly equal distribution to multiple legatees all the way to Executor discretion. That's where life can become fraught with friction, or as Ralph Waldo Emerson observed, "When it comes to divide an estate, the politest men quarrel."

Two relatives who want the portrait of Great Aunt Mary and can't agree over who deserves it more will approach you with menacing glares to demand that you decide. One way or the other, you've made an enemy . . . unless they agree to flipping a coin or you can find another item that one of the contestants (let's hope not both) wants as much as the portrait.

How about the situation where one of the deceased's fishing buddies wants his old rowboat and equally ancient boat trailer? If no one else wants it, letting the angler have it will present no problems, but what if it's a new big fancy five-figure bass boat with a hog of a motor and all the other bells and whistles? Sure, you could turn over the keys if no one else objects, but you'd be lax in your fiduciary duty: such a valuable item should be put up for sale, with the proceeds going into the estate. And even if the fisherman wants to buy the boat, he'd have by rights to pay the fair market value. That doesn't always happen—"family rates" are not unknown, but it's not what the law has in mind.

On the other hand, if a relative who is to receive an amount of money needs a medical procedure that she can't otherwise afford, giving her the money sooner than later is well within an Executor's scope of discretion, assuming there'll be enough left for taxes . . . and for the other beneficiaries under the Will. If not, Uncle Sam and everyone else won't be very happy with you.

SORTING OUT TAXES

And speaking of taxes . . . taxes to be paid by an estate's Executor are frequently thought of only as death taxes, i.e., federal and state estate taxes, but you also may have to file income tax returns for the decedent and/or the estate. It's not a matter to be taken lightly: You're personally liable for the payment of taxes if, before the estate is distributed and you are discharged as Executor, you had notice of any tax obligations or failed to exercise due diligence as to whether any obligations existed. You may also be liable for penalties or interest assessed because of late filing, undervaluation, or other deficiencies.

- Individual income tax returns: To determine whether a final income tax return is required, you must know the deceased's income. However, if he had net self-employment income of $400 or more during the taxable year to the date of his death, a final federal return must be filed regardless of the amount of gross income. Many if not most states that have income taxes require returns to be filed for the year of death, and for prior years, when returns should have been but were not.

- Fiduciary income tax returns: For income tax purposes, a decedent's probate estate is a separate entity that begins at the decedent's death. A federal Fiduciary Income Tax Return (Form 1041) must be filed for an estate with a gross income for the taxable year of $600 or more. State fiduciary tax laws vary. As a practical matter, most tax professionals prepare state fiduciary income tax returns when federal returns are required.

- Federal and state estate tax returns: The federal estate tax, which applies to all transfers of property from a decedent whether made during lifetime or at death, is based on the decedent's taxable estate, which means the gross estate less allowable deductions, reduced by allowable credits. At this time the amount of this credit reduces the computed tax so that only total taxable estates and lifetime gifts that exceed $1,000,000 will actually have to pay tax. In its current form, the estate tax only affects the wealthiest two percent of the population. Therefore, most relatively simple estates do not require an estate tax return, but filing is required for those with combined gross assets and prior taxable gifts exceeding $3,500,000, effective for decedents dying on or after January 1, 2009.

Both the federal and most state estate tax returns must be filed within nine months after the date of death unless an extension has been received. Unlike personal income taxes, an extension of time to file is not given automatically, so an application for an extension of time to file should be made to the IRS center where the return is to be filed in adequate time before the return is due, to enable the IRS to consider and reply to the application. Any extension does not extend the time for payment of the estate tax due, which must be requested separately if needed. Separate penalties may also be assessed for late filing and late payment of the tax due, in addition to interest on the late payments. The IRS may also impose an "accuracy-related penalty" if it finds that any listed assets are undervalued. It is therefore important to value the assets as accurately as possible.

Of great help is an IRS booklet, publication #559, *Information for Survivors, Executors, and Administrators*. It's available from your local IRS office. However, if the idea of handling tax matters is daunting, and it is for most nonattorneys and nonaccountants, find yourself a good tax lawyer or CPA. You and the estate's beneficiaries will be better off.

CLOSING THE ESTATE

Once you've done everything required of you, it is time to close the estate, which releases you from your legal obligation as Executor, again depending on state law. There are a few ways to do so.

The first is by filing a verified statement with the court that states that you've fully administered the estate by distributing the estate's assets to everyone entitled to them and by making payments and settlements or otherwise disposing of all claims, by paying all administration expenses, and by paying all taxes. The verified statement must be notarized.

There's usually a time limit, in that you can't file such a statement within three or four months after you were appointed Executor. Then, if no proceedings involving you are pending a year after the statement was filed, you will be discharged from your fiduciary duties. Therefore, you should be super certain that you've done everything required of you before filing the statement.

In case you were obliged to post a bond, you may want to file an application for a certificate of full administration (or whatever your state calls it). This is something of a formality, since it's unlikely that he had to post a bond as Executor. Nevertheless, some Executors feel more comfortable having a court-issued document that closes the estate.

Since nothing in many state probate statutes requires that an estate be closed, some never are. In that case, the Executor continues to have the authority to act on behalf of the estate indefinitely, but that also involves indefinite liability for actions as personal representative.

But let's say the estate was formally closed and with it your Executorship, but someone later discovered that the deceased owned a piece of property that no one knew about and that he forgot about. Or, as often happens, a doctor or another health care provider didn't get around to submitting a bill until many years later. In that event, you must petition the court (in some states a court other than the probate court) to reopen the estate and reappoint you as Executor. The court may indeed appoint you, but the judge has the discretion to name someone else. That also applies if someone discovers a mistake in the probate proceedings, such as if the title to the property was improperly transferred.

SIMPLIFIED PROCEDURES

If these full-blown full-scale probate proceedings sound daunting, you'll be happy to learn that there are alternatives. Every state has some sort of faster and easier system for distributing small estates through out-of-court procedures that transfer property directly to beneficiaries who submit affidavits, or by summary probate procedures. To be eligible, the estate must be below a certain dollar limit, ranging between $3,000 and $50,000 in most states, although a handful of states have set the limit at $100,000. Insurance proceeds, joint-tenancy, and other property that passes outside the probate procedure is excluded from computing that figure; some states exclude real estate, while others don't.

In those states that offer affidavit procedure, a surviving spouse and/or one of the heirs present a signed affidavit along with a certified death certificate to the place holding the deceased property. That might be a bank, a brokerage house, or a mutual fund, an employer if back wages are due, or the

Department of Motor Vehicles (some states also include the holder of real estate among those on whom affidavits may be served). The person or institution so served must then release the funds or property. Depending on state law, the affidavit may have to be filed with the court.

If your loved one's estate qualifies, most states require a waiting period that ranges from a month to forty-five days before you can begin this course of action. A caveat: you can't avail yourself of the procedure once the probate process has begun. The appropriate affidavit form is available as part of the statute authorizing the procedure and is downloadable after you locate the statute online (as an example, Washington State's affidavit is in Appendix D). In addition, some banks, brokerage houses, and departments of motor vehicles have the blank form on their websites.

You should be aware that not every person or institution may be willing to relinquish property only on the basis of an affidavit and a death certificate. "What about a Will?" you may be asked or may be told, "I'm not turning it over until a court says I should." Don't lose your temper; those people are just being cautious. In such case, you may have to show them the statute and assure them that there won't be any probate proceeding. However, special rules may apply to stocks and bonds held in brokerage accounts, in which you'll have to deal with a transfer agent or with other shareholders in privately held companies.

An estate that doesn't qualify for an affidavit procedure may still be eligible for summary probate, which is a court procedure but one that's far less complicated and time-consuming than full-fledged probate. As with affidavit procedures, there are dollar limitations and a one- to two-month waiting period.

Once the time period has elapsed, as Executor under the Will, you file a petition with the court to request a summary proceeding. You may also be asked to submit any or all of the following: a copy of the will, a death certificate, and an inventory and appraisal of Uncle Fred's assets. This filing can usually be done by mail, so there's no need for a personal appearance.

You can even use this procedure if there is no Will: You would ask the court to determine who receives the property under the state's intestacy laws.

In the event the judge approves, the court authorizes procedure and then removes itself, with no further judicial supervision. You then place a notice in the newspaper and send written notice to beneficiaries and creditors, since many states dispense with the notice requirement. You pay the creditors, distribute assets to Uncle Fred's beneficiaries, file a closing statement with the court once you've finished paying and distributing . . . and you've done your job.

In the case of both affidavit procedure and simplified probate, many courts provide printed or downloadable instructional materials, and most court clerks will answer your questions. Or, if you wish, retain the services of a lawyer or paralegal to look over your shoulder.

CHAPTER 8

Estate Planning

> *"Anyone may arrange his affairs so that his taxes shall be as low as possible; he is not bound to choose that pattern which best pays the treasury. There is not even a patriotic duty to increase one's taxes. Over and over again the Courts have said that there is nothing sinister in so arranging affairs as to keep taxes as low as possible. Everyone does it, rich and poor alike and all do right, for nobody owes any public duty to pay more than the law demands. . . ."*
>
> **—US Appeals Court Judge Learned Hand in**
> *Helvering v. Gregory,* **69 F.2d 809 (1934)**

Just as the best form of health care is preventative medicine, the best form of legal care when a loved one dies is through estate planning. Perhaps after all was said and done in the way of probate, your loved one's estate could have benefited from a healthy dose of proactive preplanning, but that's a matter of postmortem "too little too late." However, even if there were no hitches in his estate, you would be doing his family and friends—and you and yours too—a great favor by acquainting them with the basics of estate planning. In a very real sense, it's a gift that will keep on giving.

Estate planning is the process of organizing financial and personal assets so a person's wishes can be carried out with a minimum of inconvenience and expense. "Inconvenience" can include going through the probate system, and in that regard there are many ways to reduce the property that probate will consider. Indeed, there are ways to avoid probate entirely. As for "expense," estate planning can arrange that an estate subject to estate tax will incur the minimum possible liability.

Let's begin by considering Wills.

MAKING A WILL

You've already seen how a Will operates in the probate process, but you should know what the essential elements are. First is testamentary capacity, lawyer-talk for determining the capability to execute a legal Will. Under the Uniform Probate Code and the laws of most other states that don't use the Code, any individual eighteen or more years of age who is of sound mind may make one. As ever, there are exceptions, in this case a minor who is serving in the military may in some states be considered adult enough to make a Will.

Just what constitutes a "sound mind"? In general, the testator should be aware of his property's value, who his beneficiaries are and which ones will get what property, and how rational the plan of distribution will be (to cite an extreme example, a testator's wanting to leave everything to "that cute girl I had a crush on in grammar school if I could only remember her name after all these years" would raise serious doubts).

The idea is to protect again any unhappy beneficiaries from claiming more than their designated shares or a person was "shut out" but would take by intestacy from trying to nullify the Will. To contest a Will for lack of testamentary capacity involves proving that the testator was unable to remember close family members or had irrational opinions of them. If there's even the slightest chance of raising the issue of senility or insanity, lawyers often have the signing of the Will videotaped, during which time the testator is asked about his family, other beneficiaries, and the Will's contents.

Another option is a self-proving Will, in which the witnesses swear that they believed everything to be legally acceptable (an example of that affidavit is at the end of the Will in Appendix C).

As for witnesses, most states require two people, while others want three. Although any mentally competent adult can act as witness, choosing people who are not named as a beneficiary or Executor helps avoid any potential or alleged conflict of interest. A witness's address should be included; several states impose fines if an address doesn't accompany a signature. Even if not legally required, you should have the Will notarized.

A typical Will, such as the one that appears in Appendix C, begins with the Testator's name and a declaration that what he's executing is indeed his Last Will and Testament. Language like "bequeath, convey, and devise" that is found in many Wills may seem stilted to some people and quaint to others, but the words have acquired certain legal consequences over the centuries, the reason why lawyers continue to use them.

Then comes a paragraph about paying creditors, followed by specific bequests, and then directions about the disposition of the remainder of the estate (that is, everything else after the specific bequests). There will be a paragraph appointing the Executor or personal representative, and one about payment of taxes.

That's basically all you need for a simple Will. However, since life is rarely simple, other provisions might be included, such as custody of minor children and instructions regarding burial or cremation and organ donation.

Many married couples include a simultaneous death clause along the lines of: "If my spouse and I shall die under such circumstances that the order of our deaths cannot be readily ascertained, my spouse shall be deemed to have predeceased me. No person, other than my spouse, shall be deemed to have survived me if such person dies within thirty days after my death." The provision exists to avoid the problems that happen if both spouses perish in the same vehicle or airplane accident. Both spouses' Wills would contain an identical clause, even though both documents directing that the other spouse died first certainly seems contradictory. However, the language allows each Will to be probated by itself so the property disposition in each one will be carried out as intended. The second sentence prevents a problem when a beneficiary dies between the time the testator does and the time the estate is distributed. Instead of passing through two probates, the gift to the recently deceased beneficiary goes to the person whom the testator would have wanted it to go had the intended beneficiary died before he or she did, although most such property passes into the residuary estate.

When minor children may have to be taken care of, a provision appointing a guardian is essential: "If my spouse does not survive me and I leave minor children surviving me, I appoint as guardian of the person and property of my minor children my sister Caroline Brown, who shall have custody of my minor children, and shall serve without bond. If she does not qualify or for any reason ceases to serve as guardian, I appoint as successor guardian my best friend, Dolly Varden."

Providing for your pets is another appropriate testamentary subject. If none of your friends or relatives expresses a willingness to adopt Fido or Fluffy, you can designate an animal-rescue facility together with an amount of money to support the animal for the rest of its life. If you can't find a suitable facility, talk to your pet's veterinarian about having the vet choose a new home if your pet survives you, again with your earmarking a fund to pay for such care.

What about disinheriting a member of the family? A parent's threatening a black-sheep child, "Keep that up and I'll cut you off without a penny" is a staple of melodramatic fiction, and it can be done. To avoid a challenge to the Will with a claim that the parent overlooked a child (and therefore the Will is invalid), many estate planners recommend leaving the child a token amount of money or a gift.

Spouses are a different story. In those states that have community property laws (Alaska, Arizona, California [includes domestic partnerships as well as marriages], Idaho, Louisiana, Nevada, New Mexico, Texas, Washington, and Wisconsin), the surviving spouse is entitled to one-half of the assets (with certain exceptions), a right which cannot be defeated by disinheritance. Spouses in non-community-property states are protected by statute: The survivor must receive at least the statutory share, which is usually what he or she would inherit via intestacy.

A testamentary trust, which is a trust created by a Will, is often a sensible addition. Unlike in a living trust (which we'll get to later in this chapter), property conveyed by a testamentary trust cannot avoid probate. That's because testamentary trusts are usually intended primarily to keep large sums of money from immediately passing to minor orphans if both their parents die. Such a trust may stipulate that assets go to a surviving spouse, but in the event none exists, then to a designated Trustee on behalf of the minors until they reach a certain age (usually, but not necessarily, legal adulthood). Since state laws dictate that the trustee be subject to a probate court's supervision for the trust's duration, making testamentary trusts subject to probate is completely logical.

Not only can minors be testamentary-trust beneficiaries; other relatives (especially those who need help managing money) and friends and charities (including foundations established by the trust) can also be named. Accordingly, the testator will go to his or her reward knowing that responsible minds and hands will look after the assets until the final distribution of the estate's trust property. Banks and other financial institutions are routinely appointed trustees; not only are they experienced in handling such matters, but they exist in perpetuity, unlike human trustees who for one reason or another (for example, death) may not be able to administer the trust as long as the testator might have anticipated.

Although the trust will be subject to probate, married couples may find certain estate tax advantages. A testamentary trust creates two taxable entities: the surviving spouse and the trust, which often results in lower tax rates for both.

Since all trusts are complicated matters, the advice of a lawyer and/or accountant is highly recommended, especially with regard to avoiding or at least minimizing gift, estate, and income taxes.

How often a Will should be reviewed with an eye toward changing any provisions depends on the testator's situation. Marriage or divorce, the birth of a child, and the death of any beneficiary would be reason enough. So would a beneficiary's falling out of favor or changed circumstances. Case in point: Someone who seemed like a prime candidate for the poorhouse, and for whom several relatives made testamentary provisions, suddenly hit the lottery for big bucks, whereupon his relatives revised their Wills—and hoped that Mr. Lucky wouldn't forget them in his Will.

Even if there hasn't been any such a signal event, lawyers and estate planners often suggest reviewing the document every five years; just looking at the provisions may give you occasion to reflect and possibly take action.

Now that you have a Will, let's find ways to keep your assets out of your estate, and in ways that your Executor may never have to file the Will for probate. There's nothing that says a Will must be probated, especially if savvy estate planning provides your beneficiaries with your assets by other means.

Living Trusts

A trust is a device by which someone holds property for the benefit of another person. A living trust (also called an *inter vivos* trust from the Latin for "among the living") is a trust created when the settlor—that's the trust-creator, sometimes called the grantor—is alive. It's a very useful mechanism that lets your assets be distributed easily and quickly after your death without having to make use of the probate process. If privacy is a consideration, a living trust is better than a Will in that it isn't registered with or revealed in a probate court. And if, heaven forbid, you become incapacitated, a living trust can authorize someone else to manage your affairs, or at least those that are included in the trust.

Putting your property into a trust means that the trust legally owns that property. However, and here's the best part, you don't have to relinquish any control whatsoever if you don't want to. As grantor, you will usually appoint yourself to be the trust's initial trustee (a "trustee" manages the trust), which means you still have complete power over the corpus (the body of the trust). You can add to or sell all or part . . . whatever you could do if there were no trust, such as real estate (including time-shares), businesses (entirely or your portion of the ownership), investment securities, and works of art. And since at some point you might change your mind about the whole idea, you can create a revocable trust that you can terminate whenever you wish.

Some items, however, cannot or should not be placed in trust. IRAs and 401(k)s, for example, cannot because they must be held by real people, not the artificial entity that is a trust. Life insurance proceeds go directly to the beneficiary, so there's no reason to include the policy unless the beneficiary is someone, like a minor, who needs the protection of a fiduciary. Then too, it makes little sense to place items that you buy and sell frequently—for example, you collect antique firearms, some of which you trade for other weapons—in a trust since you'd have to redo the trust instrument every time you acquired or sold something. (There are also reasons why you don't have to include property that would otherwise pass on after your death to your beneficiaries by such operation of law as joint tenancy, which we'll encounter later in this chapter.)

To sell property that you placed in a living trust, you can either sell it directly from the trust or, if the buyer insists, you as trustee transfer the property out of the trust and back to you as an individual and then sell it.

Several issues concerning real estate that will go into a living trust may call for the professional advice of a lawyer or accountant. These include the possible requirement to have the property reassessed, tax liability on the sale of the property, and something called homestead rights.

There are three categories of beneficiaries of a living trust. A primary beneficiary (or beneficiaries, since there can be more than one) receives specific property, such as real estate or a stock portfolio or a valuable painting or indeed the entire trust corpus. An alternate beneficiary gets the property if the primary beneficiary dies first. A residuary beneficiary, like the residuary beneficiary of a Will, gets all property that hasn't been left to either the primary or alternate beneficiaries. In most cases, you can choose a person or institution (such as a charity or a foundation) to be the beneficiary or beneficiaries.

As for designating your surviving spouse as a beneficiary, you'd want to make sure that he or she will get, depending on state law, one-third to one-half of your property. This will also assure the ability to claim the marital deduction under federal estate tax law, thereby reducing estate tax liability. Talk to your lawyer about ways to maximize this deduction.

You can leave property to children, too. If you desire, you can put property in trust and designate an adult to manage it on behalf of a minor. That's known as a subtrust, which will terminate when the child is no long a minor or after a stipulated event such as graduation from college or marriage. Bear in mind that such a trustee isn't the child's guardian, who can be named only in a traditional Will that will be subject to probate. A living trust can also be a vehicle for designating future care for your pets; see the suggestions in that regard in this chapter's section on writing a Will.

Creating a trust is simplicity itself. You, or a lawyer or legal paraprofessional, if you wish, will draw up a document called a "Deed of Trust" in which you as settlor list your property and then convey your ownership of it to the trustee (who has indicated that he or she will serve). Sample language of the core provision and a revocability clause can be found in Appendix E. After having the document notarized, keep it in a safe place; the trustee might want a copy, too.

Estate planners recommend that if you include an "incapacity" clause to permit a trustee to manage your affairs should you become physically or mentally unable to do so, then you should also execute a Durable Power of Attorney designating your trustee to act on your behalf on matters that are above and beyond the scope of the living trust. Despite the document's name, the trustee needn't be a lawyer. A Power of Attorney for Health Care and Living Will to cover medical considerations, especially matters of life and death, would also be a good thing to have.

Like a Will, a living trust should be reviewed periodically, and it should be amended when the settlor marries or remarries or has a child, and when a spouse, a major beneficiary, or the trustee (if not the settlor) dies. Moving to a state that has different property laws is cause for review. And divorce is a very good reason for revoking the document.

Amending or revoking a trust is just as easy as creating one: A signed and notarized document setting forth the amendments (e.g., an oil painting that was held in trust for Cousin Vincent will now go to Cousin Pablo) or declaring that the trust is hereby revoked is how it's done. However, be aware that certain tax consequences may ensue, so check first with your lawyer or accountant if you have any questions.

Already-wealthy beneficiaries often take advantage of something called disclaimer or renunciation (lawyers and accountants refer to it as "postmortem estate planning"). If such a beneficiary would rather have property that would otherwise pass to him go directly to an alternate beneficiary, he can renounce the property within a prescribed time; the property would then pass to the residual estate or trust corpus. However, to take possession of it and then change your mind constitutes a taxable event. Disclaimer has primarily gift tax implications, but it also has estate tax consequences down the road, so be sure to consult with your lawyer or accountant first.

OTHER STRATEGIES

Although Wills and living trusts are vehicles that must be created, you may already have existing arrangements by which assets are transferable at and/or before death.

Retirement accounts, such as IRAs and 401(k)s, are such assets. Plans require you to name a beneficiary who will automatically receive the death benefits without their being subjected to probate. You'll want to see whether your plans allow you to name an alternate beneficiary, since some plans don't. Since state laws often protect spouses if a nonspouse is named beneficiary, you'd want to get your spouse's written consent if you've another beneficiary, such as a child or parent, in mind. Similarly, certain 401(k) plans earmark all their proceeds to a surviving spouse unless the survivor specifically waives his or her right to the money.

Stocks, bonds, and other securities can pass to a beneficiary by means of Transfer on Death Registration. The beneficiary simply claims one or more security or the proceeds from its or their sale. As usual, there are exceptions: several states don't recognize this type of transference, and in those states that do, brokerage houses can't be forced to transfer the securities or proceeds this way—they merely have the option to do so. There may be restrictions on alternate beneficiaries (government bonds allow only one beneficiary), and community property laws may affect such transfers to anyone but a surviving spouse.

A bank account is simplicity itself to "leave" to someone. The mechanism is called a Totten trust (named for a party to a 1904 case that upheld such an arrangement). It's not really a trust, but merely a garden-variety account with one or more beneficiaries designated to receive whatever proceeds remain in the account at the time the owner dies. Until then, the owner has complete control of the account, and if there's nothing left in it at the end, well, so be it.

A Totten trust is created by opening an account in that manner or changing an existing account; the bank has the form. If you don't want a minor child to come into a lot of money and blow it all on video games, you can name a custodian to receive the proceeds and manage them in a more sensible fashion on the youngster's behalf.

To change beneficiaries, you can close the account and make a new one or, less complicated, change the beneficiaries by following the bank's procedures.

Transfer on Death Registration for cars, trucks, and other vehicles is available in a handful of states—California, Connecticut, Kansas, Missouri, and Ohio. No alternate beneficiaries are allowed, though. Papers are filed with the Department of Motor Vehicles, from whom the surviving beneficiary will obtain registration papers in his or her name.

The real property equivalent, Transfer on Death Deeds, is available in Arizona, Arkansas, Colorado, Kansas, Missouri, Montana, New Mexico, Ohio, and Wisconsin. The landowner records a deed that doesn't take effect until the death of the landowner, or if a joint tenancy, the last surviving owner. The beneficiary then files an affidavit and a death certificate, at which point a new deed is issued in his or her name. Such deeds are revocable; the options are recording a notarized revocation, recording a new deed with no mention of a transfer-on-death benefit, or by transferring or selling the property.

A piece of real property may be transferred on death by operation of law (attorney-talk for "automatically") if the property is held in joint tenancy. That phrase has nothing to do with being a tenant; it comes from the Latin word for "hold"; the joint tenant holds the property together with one or more other people. A joint tenancy, which is created by two or more people acquiring property (and not just real estate) together, includes the right of survivorship—the property automatically passes to the surviving joint tenant(s). The marital equivalent is called tenancy by the entirety; the surviving spouse acquires the property by operation of law.

PLAN AHEAD FOR THE INEVITABLE

No one likes to contemplate death, especially his or her own, but we must acknowledge that the event will eventually happen, and perhaps sooner than hoped for. That's why an integral part of estate planning should include actively participating in ways that will make the job of those friends and family members who might survive you as painless as possible. (The same advice applies to friends and relatives who might need a gentle, if not a firm, nudge from you in that direction.)

Have you ever given any thought to where you would like done with your remains? That is to say, have you decided whether you want to be buried, and if so, where? Or would you rather be cremated, and if so, what would you like done with your ashes? Sit down with your spouse or partner and any children or a close friend or your lawyer if you're unattached, and share your decision. Remember that in the case of cemeteries, your family and will be the ones who will visit your grave, so if you've no particular resting place in mind, inspecting one or more cemeteries in their company is not a bad idea. Listen to their suggestions, which will probably include their traveling time. The same suggestion applies to columbaria if you want your ashes placed in a niche instead of being buried or scattered (unless you wish to avail yourself of a cemetery's scattering garden).

During your inspection visits, the cemetery's office can give you a map of available plots, or someone on the staff can guide you around the grounds. The prices of plots vary, so be sure to ask to see the full range of available spots. If other family members want to be buried together, you'll save money by buying more than one plot at the same time. Just as inquiring in advance about fees in other areas of estate planning—legal, accounting, and funeral homes—ask here about any opening, closing or any other fees.

Once you've decided on your resting place, turn your attention to the sort of funeral or memorial service you'd like to have. The suggestions in Chapter 3 are a useful starting place. Write down your ideas, and keep the instructions with your Will if you don't include them in the document itself.

According to AARP, in 2001 (the latest year for which figures are available), the average cost of a basic traditional adult funeral was $5,160, with burial, flowers, cards, and other items almost doubling that figure. The cost has certainly increased over the decade, so you may want to look into a prepaid funeral and burial contract. The idea is that making arrangements in advance ensures that your wishes are carried out and that funeral costs won't impose a financial burden on your survivors. Most states require funeral homes to deposit the proceeds of prepaid funeral contracts into special trust accounts to prevent commingling the money from the funeral home's other accounts (such accounts guard against embezzlement and protect your money from creditors if the funeral home goes bankrupt or completely out of business).

A prepaid funeral contract not only removes the guesswork from your survivors' having to plan your funeral, but it's a hedge against inevitable increases in funeral costs, although some contracts require survivors to pay additional amounts—yet another reason to shop around and read the contract closely. In that regard, you'll also want to ask about exactly what the contract covers, whether you will have the funeral and the cemetery of your choice, and whether the contract can be canceled if you subsequently change your mind (perhaps you will move to another part of the country or you'll marry or remarry someone who had different ideas about where you or she will rest forever).

Another advantage that may be relevant to your situation is that the cost of a prepaid funeral contract is not included in computing Medicaid eligibility, another way to avoid making surviving family members pay for your funeral.

However, keep in mind that the cost of a prepaid funeral contract is not inexpensive, and you may be able to invest the money on your own in such a way that its returns will cover your funeral cost with money to spare.

In conclusion, and once again, making the decisions and taking the actions described in this chapter will give you and loved ones the peace of mind that is among the greatest gifts of love that are yours to give and to share.

A Checklist

(with reference to page numbers)

___ Notify survivors   3–4

___ Notify deceased's employer   4–5

___ Locate Will and any organ donation card   5

___ Provide care for orphaned minors and pets   6

___ Stop newspaper delivery and other daily services   6

___ Cancel credit and charge cards   6–7

___ Secure deceased's residence   7–8

___ Contact funeral home   12

___ Help fill out death certificate information   13

___ Answer funeral director's questions about deceased's remains and wishes for service   14–24

___ Compose obituary   24–26

Probate:

A Checklist

Alternates to probate:

___ Simplified affidavit procedure   99–101

___ Summary probate procedure   100–101

Estate planning:

___ Make a Will   104–110

___ Establish a living trust   111–115

___ Make alternate conveyances   115–118

___ Plan for your future   118–121

125

Funeral Practices

The purpose of this material is to describe the funeral practices of major faiths in general terms. Because there can be variations even within the same denomination or group, anyone who is making funeral arrangements for someone of another faith and who is unfamiliar with such practices should consult with a leader, if any, of the deceased's religious community.

BUDDHISM

A funeral ceremony in several Japanese Buddhist traditions resembles a Christian ceremony in the West, with a eulogy and prayers at a funeral home.

Cambodian, Thai, and Sri Lankan traditions may have up to three ceremonies. The first, held within two days after death, is conducted by monks at the home of the bereaved. In the second, which takes place within two to five days after death, monks conduct a service at a funeral home. There is always an open casket at the main ceremony and the guests are encouraged to view the body, as Buddhism considers the viewing as a valuable reminder of the transitory nature of life. Guests are expected to make a slight bow toward the body. Seven days after burial or cremation is the third ceremony either at the home of the bereaved or at a temple. It is called a "merit transference" and generates energy for the deceased's incarnation.

All Buddhist traditions and sects quote from the Sutras, which are the collected sayings of the Buddha.

In the Tibetan tradition, a dying or recently deceased person will have certain religious literature read to them to guide them through the *bardo* transition period toward spiritual enlightenment. As the *bardo* is generally said to last a maximum of forty-nine days, these readings and other rituals will usually last forty-nine days. Accordingly, it is advisable to consult with the deceased's *sangha*, or fellow practitioners, so that they may begin the appropriate rituals before, during, and after death.

CHURCH OF CHRIST, SCIENTIST

The Church of Christ, Scientist, does not designate special arrangements or rituals for funerals or mourning. Any service is conducted by a Christian Scientist who might be a reader, practitioner (healer), teacher, or a friend of the deceased. A service typically consists of readings from the King James Bible and from *Science and Health with Key to the Scriptures* or some other writing by Mary Baker Eddy, the faith's founder. Any personal remarks or eulogy are in accordance with the family's wishes. There is no customary period of mourning.

GREEK ORTHODOX CHURCH

The Greek Orthodox funeral ceremony is not part of a larger service (as is the Roman Catholic mass). An open casket is traditional, as are mourners bowing in front of the casket and kissing an icon or cross that has been placed on the deceased's chest. At the graveside prayer ceremony, each person present places a flower on the casket. A memorial service is held on the Sunday closest to the fortieth day after the death.

It is customary to comfort the bereaved with "May you have an abundant life" or "May their memory be eternal."

HINDUISM

The body remains at home until taken to the place of cremation, which is usually twenty-four hours after death. It is customary to wear white clothing at the funeral. Hindu priests or older male family members recite mantras. At the cremation ceremony, called the *mukhagni*, a last food offering is symbolically made to the deceased, after which the body is cremated. A *shraddha* ceremony is held ten days after the death of members of the Brahmin caste and thirty days for other castes. Performed at home, it is intended to liberate the soul of the deceased for its ascent to heaven.

ISLAM

Burial takes place as soon after death as practicable, the same day if possible. The family or other members of the community wash and shroud the body in sheets of clean, white cloth. The deceased is then transported to a place where funeral prayers are said, usually outdoors or in a mosque courtyard (but not inside the mosque). An imam leads the funeral prayer, which is similar in structure to Islam's five daily prayers, but without bowing or prostration; the entire prayer is said silently except for a few words.

While all members of the community attend the funeral prayers, only males accompany the body to the gravesite. The deceased is laid in the grave (without a coffin if permitted by local law) on his or her right side, facing Mecca. Tombstones, elaborate markers, or flowers or other mementos are not permitted.

The three-day mourning period is marked by prayer and receiving visitors who express condolences. Wearing jewelry and decorative clothing is not appropriate.

JUDAISM

Jewish funerals occur within twenty-four hours of death, although Orthodox Jews often bury their own before sundown of the day of death. Custom dictates that the body not be left unattended or be disturbed by autopsy (unless absolutely required by law), embalming, or cosmetic enhancement.

Funerals do not take place during the sabbath, beginning at sundown on Friday and ending at sundown on Saturday. Open caskets are not permitted in all but Reform services, and even then rarely seen.

Whether the service takes place in a synagogue, a funeral home, or at the graveside, the rabbi or cantor will recite the 23 Psalm ("The Lord is my Shepherd") and chant the *El Mole Rachamin* ("God, full of mercy") prayer. A eulogy by the officiating member of the clergy and remarks by family and friends are permissible and often encouraged.

Flowers are never appropriate for Orthodox, Conservative, and Reconstructionist services, but are often seen at Reform ones.

At the graveside, the rabbi or cantor recites prayers and leads the family in the mourner's *kaddish*, or prayer for the deceased. Everyone is encouraged to help fill in the grave with a shovelful or handful of earth. Family members leave the gravesite by passing between two rows of the others in attendance.

More traditional Jews observe a seven-day mourning period after the funeral, known as *shivah* (one "sits shivah"). Reform Jews may choose to sit for only one or two days. *Shivah* is suspended during the Sabbath.

131

Each anniversary of the death is called the *yahrzeit* at which time the family lights a candle that burns for twenty-four hours in a small glass.

CHURCH OF JESUS CHRIST OF LATTER-DAY SAINTS

A Mormon funeral follows the pattern of a sacrament meeting: an opening song, followed by an opening prayer, welcome by the presiding priesthood, addresses, a closing song, and a closing prayer. A bishop or branch president who conducts the funeral customarily invites individuals to speak and directs the program.

PROTESTANTISM

The wide variety of ways that Protestant denominations conduct funerals—from Episcopalian formal rites to Unitarian memorial services—makes generalizing especially difficult, but all the ceremonies can be said to put importance on the family's wishes with regard to prayers and music. The ceremonies celebrate the life of the deceased and often emphasize a Christian belief in everlasting life for deserving souls. Protestant funerals may be held at a church, a funeral home, graveside, or crematorium, and will consist of prayers, one or more eulogies, music, and Biblical scripture readings.

ROMAN CATHOLIC CHURCH

The evening before the funeral will be a Vigil, also known as a "wake" or "watch" in the presence of the deceased at the church or funeral home. Prayers are offered, especially the Rosary, and a eulogy may be given at that time instead of during the funeral service.

A Roman Catholic funeral is done as a mass called a "Rite of Christian Burial," identical to other masses except for the presence of the casket, which the priest who celebrates the mass meets at the church door and escorts up the aisle. The celebrant's homily customarily also makes reference to the deceased in the context of the Gospel read during the service.

Following the funeral mass is the Rite of Committal at the grave or crematorium. That service consists of the prayer of committal, a Scriptural verse, intercession, the Lord's Prayer, and a blessing.

THE RELIGIOUS SOCIETY OF FRIENDS

A Quaker funeral, or memorial meeting, is either "unprogrammed" or "programmed." Unprogrammed meetings are held in the traditional manner of a Friends service where worshippers sit and wait for divine guidance and inspiration. If so moved, they then speak to the group.

Programmed meetings are planned in advance. They may include hymn singing, spoken prayers, Bible reading, silent worship, and a sermon. In many cases, worship is led by a pastor.

SIKHISM

A short ceremony takes place at the funeral home before the cremation. An *ardas*, or community prayer, is recited to begin the service. Two Sikh daily prayers, the *Japji Sahib* and *Kirtan*

Sohila, are recited and the cremation begins. Although these prayers may be continuously recited throughout the cremation, the basic funeral service ends at this time and guests may leave.

Afterward, there may be another service at the *gurdwara*, the Sikh place of worship, but this is optional. Traditionally, the word "akal," which means "undying," is chanted at this service to help release the soul to return to the infinite. For gurdwara services, everyone sits on the floor facing the Guru Granth Sahib, the Sikh holy writings, sometimes with the men on the left and the women on the right.

A Sample Basic Will

Last Will And Testament

I, Frederick Long Green, residing at 400 Elm Street, Hometown, East Carolina 80001, declare this to be my Will, and I revoke any and all Wills and codicils I previously executed.

ARTICLE I: Funeral expenses & payment of debt

I direct my Executors to pay my enforceable unsecured debts and funeral expenses, the expenses of my last illness, and the expenses of administering my estate.

ARTICLE II: Money & Personal Property

A. Subject to the specific bequests enumerated hereunder, I give all my tangible personal property and all policies and proceeds of insurance covering such property, to my granddaughter Susan. If she does not survive me, I give that property to those of my nieces and nephews who survive me, in equal shares, to be divided among them by my Executors in their absolute discretion. My Executors may pay out of my estate the expenses of delivering tangible personal property to beneficiaries.

B. I give the sum of One Thousand Dollars ($1,000.00) in equal shares to my nieces and nephews living at the time of my death. If any shall not survive me, his or her share shall be given in equal shares to those who survive me.

C. I give the sum of One Thousand Dollars ($1,000.00) to the Hometown Community Church for its unrestricted use.

D. I give the grandfather's clock in the living room to my nephew John.

E. I give my fishing tackle and boat to my good friend, Ike Walton.

ARTICLE III: Real Estate

I give all my residences, subject to any mortgages or encumbrances thereon, and all policies and proceeds of insurance covering such property, to my granddaughter Susan. If she does not survive me, I direct that the properties be sold and the proceeds given in equal shares to my nieces and nephews living at the time of my death. If any shall not survive me, his or her share shall be given in equal shares to those who survive me.

ARTICLE IV: Residuary Clause

I give the rest, residue and remainder of my estate to my granddaughter, Susan. If she does not survive me, I give my residuary estate to those of my nieces and nephews who survive me, in equal shares.

ARTICLE V: Taxes

I direct my Executors, without apportionment against any beneficiary or other person, to pay all estate, inheritance, and succession taxes (including any interest and penalties thereon) payable by reason of my death.

ARTICLE VI: Minors

If any property under this Will shall be payable outright to a person who is a minor, my Executors may, without court approval, pay all or part of such property to a parent or guardian of that minor, to a custodian under the Uniform Transfers to Minors act, or may defer payment of such property until the minor reaches the age of majority.

ARTICLE VII: Fiduciaries

I appoint my nephew, Joseph Smith, as Executor of this Will. If he is unable or unwilling to act or if he resigns, I appoint my attorney, Oliver Mendel Holmes, as successor. My Executor shall have all the powers allowable to Executors under the laws of this state. I direct that no bond or security of any kind shall be required of any Executor.

I have signed this Will on this 30th day of February 2010.

_____

[legal signature]

SIGNED AND DECLARED by Frederick Long Green on [date] to be his will, in our presence, who at his request, in his presence and in the presence of each other, all being present at the same time, have signed our names as witnesses.

Ima Watchin [signature]

Witness: Ima Watchin

Address: 64 Longview Ave, Hometown, East Carolina 80002

Esau Watchin [signature]

Witness: Esau Watchin

Address: 64 Longview Ave, Hometown, East Carolina 80002

Self-Proving Affidavit

STATE OF EAST CAROLINA

COUNTY OF STONEWALL

Each of the undersigned, Ima Watchin and Esau Watchin, both on oath, says that:

The attached will was signed by Fredrick Long Green, the testator named in the Will, on this 30th day of February, 2010 at the law offices of Oliver Mendel Holmes, Esq., 765 Main St., Hometown, East Carolina 80003.

When he signed the Will, Frederick Long Green declared the instrument to be his last Will.

Each of us then signed his or her name as a witness at the end of this Will at the request of Frederick Long Green and in his presence and sight and in the presence and sight of each other.

Frederick Long Green was, at the time of executing this Will, over the age of eighteen years and, in our opinions, of sound mind, memory, and understanding and not under any restraint or in any respect incompetent to make a Will.

In our opinions, Frederick Long Green could read, write, and speak in English and was suffering from no physical or mental impairment that would affect his capacity to make a valid Will. The Will was executed as a single original instrument, and was not executed in counterparts.

Each of us was acquainted with Frederick Long Green when the Will was executed and makes this affidavit at his request.

Both witnesses were present at the same time, have signed our names as witnesses.

Ima Watchin [signature]

Witness: Ima Watchin

Esau Watchin [signature]

Witness: Esau Watchin

Sworn to before me this 30th day of February, 2010

Maynard G. Krebbs

Notary Public [signature and official seal]

Small Estate Affidavit

STATE OF WASHINGTON

Estate of
GEORGE WASHINGTON

SMALL ESTATE
AFFIDAVIT (RCW 11.62.010)

Deceased

Having been sworn under oath, I declare as follows:

1. **Decedent's Death Certificate.** A copy of Decedent's Death Certificate is attached to this Affidavit.

2. **Forty Days Since Death.** Forty (40) or more days have elapsed since Decedent's death.

3. **Washington Resident.** Decedent was a resident of Washington at his/her death.

4. **No Personal Representative.** No application or petition for the appointment of a Personal Representative is pending or has been granted in any jurisdiction.

5. **Decedent's Net Probate Estate Does Not Exceed $100,000.** The value of Decedent's entire estate subject to probate, not including any surviving spouse's community property interest in such assets, wherever located, less liens and encumbrances, does not exceed one hundred thousand dollars ($100,000).

6. **Decedent's Debts.** All of Decedent's debts, including funeral and burial expenses, have been paid or provided for.

7. **My Name & Address.** My name and address are as shown below.

8. **Claiming Successor.** I am a "successor" of Decedent as defined in RCW 11.62.005.

9. **Other Claiming Successors.**

   No Others. I am the only claiming Successor; there are no others.

   —— OR ——

   Other Claiming Successors. There are other claiming Successors. I have given each of them written notice, by personal service or mail, identifying my claim and describing the property claimed. At least ten (10) days have elapsed since the service or mailing of such notice.

10. Entitlement to Property.

Sole Entitlement. I am personally entitled to full payment or delivery of the property claimed.

—— OR ——

Entitlement on Behalf of All Claiming Successors. I am personally entitled to full payment or delivery of the property claimed on behalf, and with the written authority, of all other claiming Successors; a copy of which authority is attached to this Affidavit.

11. Property Claimed. A description of the personal property claimed, all of which is subject to probate, is as follows:

Dated:

*Signature:*_____
Decedent's Claiming Successor

Printed Name:

Address:

143

The Primary Provision of a Living Trust

Agreement made and executed this _____ day of _____, 20___ by and between _____, hereinafter referred to as the Settlor, and _____, hereinafter referred to as the Trustee.

Settlor desires to create a revocable trust of the property described in Schedule A hereto annexed, together with such monies, and other assets as the Trustee may hereafter at any time hold or acquire hereunder (hereinafter referred to collectively as the "Trust Estate") for the purposes hereinafter set forth.

NOW, THEREFORE, in consideration of the premises and of the mutual covenants herein contained, the Settlor agrees to execute such further instruments as shall be necessary to vest the Trustee with full title to the property, and the Trustee agrees to hold the Trust Estate, IN TRUST, NEVERTHELESS, for the following uses and purposes and subject to the terms and conditions hereinafter set forth:

The Trustee shall hold, manage, invest, and reinvest the Trust Estate (if any requires such management and investment) and shall collect the income, if any, therefrom and shall dispose of the net income and principal as follows:

(1) During the lifetime of the Settlor, the Trustee shall pay to or apply for the benefit of the Settlor all the net income from the Trust.

(2) During the lifetime of the Settlor, the Trustee may pay to or apply for the benefit of the Settlor such sums from the principal of this Trust as in its sole discretion shall be necessary or advisable from time to time for the medical care, comfortable maintenance and welfare of the Settlor, taking into consideration to the extent the Trustee deems advisable, any other income or resources of the Settlor known to the Trustee.

(3) The Settlor may at any time during his/her lifetime and from time to time, withdraw all or part of the principal of this Trust, free of trust, by delivering an instrument in writing duly signed by him/her to the Trustee, describing the property or portion thereof desired to be withdrawn. Upon receipt of such instrument, the Trustee shall thereupon convey and deliver to the Settlor, free of trust, the property described in such instrument.

(4) In the event that the Settlor is adjudicated to be incompetent or in the event that the Settlor is not adjudicated incompetent, but by reason of illness or mental or physical disability is, in the opinion of the Trustee, unable to properly handle his/her own affairs, then and in that event the Trustee may during the Settlor's lifetime, in addition to the payments of income and principal for the benefit of the Settlor, pay to or apply for the benefit of the Settlor's spouse, and of any one or more of Settlor's minor children, such sums from the net income and from the principal of this Trust in such shares and proportions as in its sole discretion it shall determine to be necessary or advisable from time to time for the medical care, comfortable

maintenance, and welfare of the Settlor's said spouse and children taking into consideration to the extent the Trustee deems advisable, any other income or resources of the Settlor's said spouse and minor children known to the Trustee.

(5) The interests of the Settlor shall be considered primary and superior to the interests of any beneficiary.

II

The Settlor reserves and shall have the exclusive right any time and from time to during his/her lifetime by instrument in writing signed by the Settlor and delivered to the Trustee to modify or alter this Agreement, in whole or in part, without the consent of the Trustee or any beneficiary provided that the duties, powers, and liabilities of the Trustee shall not be changed without his/her consent; and the Settlor reserves and shall have the right during his/her lifetime, by instrument in writing, signed by the Settlor and delivered to the Trustee, to cancel and annul this Agreement without the consent of the Trustee or any beneficiary hereof. Settlor expressly reserves the right to appoint successor trustees, replace present trustees, and change the beneficiaries or the rights to property due any beneficiary.

A Bouquet of Quotations

You may find some of these quotations comforting and perhaps sufficiently relevant to how you feel about your loved one to serve as an inspiration for a eulogy.

"Perhaps the best cure for the fear of death is to reflect that life has a beginning as well as an end. There was a time when we were not: this gives us no concern—why then should it trouble us that a time will come when we shall cease to be?"
—William Hazlitt

149

"As a well-spent day brings happy sleep, so life well used brings happy death."

—Leonardo da Vinci

"O death, where is thy sting? O grave, where is thy victory?"

—First Corinthians

"In the night of death, hope sees a star, and listening love can hear the rustle of a wing."

—Robert Ingersoll

"Do not seek death. Death will find you.
But seek the road which makes death a fulfillment."

—Dag Hammarskjöld

"It is foolish and wrong to mourn the men who died.
Rather we should thank God that such men lived."

—General George S. Patton Jr.

"Good men must die, but death cannot kill their names."

—Proverbs

"Death's truer name
Is 'Onward,' no discordance in the roll

And march of that Eternal Harmony
Whereto the world beats time."

—Alfred, Lord Tennyson

"Let's choose Executors and talk of wills.
And yet not so—for what can we bequeath,
Save our deposed bodies to the ground?"

—Shakespeare

"Life does not cease to be funny when people die any
more than it ceases to be serious when people laugh."

—George Bernard Shaw

"Is a man a
    morning glory that he passes
    in a day?"

—Japanese haiku

"That best portion of a good man's life,
His little, nameless, unremembered acts
Of kindness and of love."

—William Wordsworth

"There is no cure for birth and death save to enjoy the
interval."

—George Santayana

"Perhaps they are not the stars,
But rather openings in heaven where
The love of our lost ones pours through
And shines down upon us to let us know they are happy."

—Inuit sentiment

"Alas for those that never sing,
But die with all their music in them!"

—Oliver Wendell Holmes

"Death is a commingling of eternity with time; in the death of a good man, eternity is seen looking through time."

—Johann Wolfgang von Goethe

"Sometimes, when one person is absent, the whole world seems depopulated."

—Alphonse de Lamartine

"You can clutch the past so tightly to your chest that it leaves your arms too full to embrace the present."

—Jan Glidewell

"God pours life into death and death into life without a drop being spilled."

—Anonymous

"I'm not afraid of death. It's the stake one puts up in order to play the game of life."

—Jean Giraudoux

"Say not in grief: 'He is no more,'
but live in thankfulness that he was."

—Hebrew proverb

"A death is not the extinguishing of a light,
but the putting out of the lamp
because the dawn has come . . .
Let the dead have the immortality of fame,
but the living the immortality of love."

—Rabindranath Tagore

"Let us endeavor to live so that when we come to die even the undertaker will be sorry."

—Mark Twain

"For everything there is a season
And a time for every matter under heaven:
A time to be born, and a time to die;
A time to plant, and a time to pluck up what is planted;
A time to kill, and a time to heal;
A time to break down, and a time to build up;
A time to weep, and a time to laugh;

A time to mourn, and a time to dance;

A time to throw away stones, and a time to gather stones together;

A time to embrace, And a time to refrain from embracing;

A time to seek, and a time to lose;

A time to keep, and a time to throw away;

A time to tear, and a time to sew;

A time to keep silence, and a time to speak;

A time to love, and a time to hate,

A time for war, and a time for peace."

—Ecclesiastes 3:1–8

"Don't cry because it's over. Smile because it happened."

—Dr. Seuss

"While we are mourning the loss of our friend, others are rejoicing to meet him behind the veil."

—John Taylor

"He who has gone, so we but cherish his memory, abides with us, more potent, nay, more present than the living man."

—Antoine de Saint-Exupéry

"The greatest thing in life is to die young but to take as long a time as possible to do it."

—George Bernard Shaw

"We must embrace pain and burn it as fuel for our journey."

—Kenji Miyazawa

❧❀❧

"Death is a challenge. It tells us not to waste time. . . . It tells us to tell each other right now that we love each other."

—Leo Buscaglia

❧❀❧

"To live in hearts we leave behind is not to die."

—Clyde Campbell

❧❀❧

"If you suppress grief too much, it can well redouble."

—Molière

❧❀❧

"To laugh often and love much; to win the respect of intelligent persons and the affection of children; to earn the approbation of honest critics and to endure the betrayal of false friends; to appreciate beauty; to find the best in others; to give of one's self; to leave the world a little better, whether by a healthy child, a garden patch, or a redeemed social condition; to have played and laughed with enthusiasm and sung with exultation; to know that even one life has breathed easier because you have lived—this is to have succeeded."

—Ralph Waldo Emerson

❧❀❧

"Only in the agony of parting do we look into the depths of love."

—George Eliot

⚜

"Do not grieve me too much . . . death is only an incident, and not the most important which happens to us in this state of being. On the whole, and since I have met you, my darling one, I have been happy . . . If there is any-where else, I shall be on the lookout for you. Meanwhile look forward, feel free, rejoice in Life."

—Winston Churchill, in a letter to his wife,
written before leaving for World War I
and to be opened in the
event of his death

⚜

I come into the peace of wild things/ who do not tax their lives with forethought/ of grief. I come into the pres-ence of still water./ And I feel above me the day-blind stars/ waiting with their light. For a time/ I rest in the grace of the world, and am free."

—Wendell Berry

⚜

"Let children walk with Nature, let them see the beau-tiful blendings and communions of death and life, their joyous inseparable unity, as taught in woods and meadows, plains and mountains and streams of our blessed star, and they will learn that death is stingless indeed, and as beautiful as life."

—John Muir

"The joy in life is to be used for a purpose. I want to be used up when I die."

—George Bernard Shaw

"For death is no more than a turning of us over from time to eternity."

—William Penn

"The courage of life is often a less dramatic spectacle than the courage of the final moment; but it is no less a magnificent mixture of triumph and tragedy."

—John Fitzgerald Kennedy

"Unable are the Loved to die
For Love is Immortality."

—Emily Dickinson

"Our fear of death is like our fear that summer will be short, but when we have had our swing of pleasure, our fill of fruit, and our swelter of heat, we say we have had our day."

—Ralph Waldo Emerson

"Expect trouble as an inevitable part of life
and repeat to yourself, the most comforting words of all:
This, too, shall pass."

—Ann Landers

"Death leaves a heartache no one can heal, love leaves a
memory no one can steal."

—Engraved on a headstone in an Irish cemetery

"Do not go gentle into that good night,
Old age should burn and rave at close of day;
Rage, rage against the dying of the light.

Though wise men at their end know dark is right,
Because their words had forked no lightning they
Do not go gentle into that good night."

—Dylan Thomas

"Remember me when I am gone away,
Gone far away into the silent land;
When you can no more hold me by the hand,
Nor I half turn to go, yet turning stay.

Remember me when no more day by day
You tell me of our future that you plann'd:
Only remember me; you understand
It will be late to counsel then or pray.

Yet if you should forget me for a while
And afterwards remember, do not grieve:
For if the darkness and corruption leave
A vestige of the thoughts that once I had,
Better by far you should forget and smile
Than that you should remember and be sad."

—Christina Rossetti

Glossary

administrator: A court-appointed person or institution put in charge of the estate of a person who died intestate.

affidavit: A written declaration sworn under oath before a notary public or other authorized official.

arrangement room: A room or office in the funeral home where the funeral director and the bereaved make funeral arrangements.

attorney in fact: Any person granted the power of attorney.

beneficiary: The recipient of the proceeds of a Will or an insurance policy.

bequest: A gift of property made in a Will. Another word for "legacy."

bereaved: The immediate family of the deceased and others who mourn the deceased.

bond: A guaranty by an insurance or similar company agreeing to compensate any financial loss by an Executor, administrator, trustee, or other fiduciary.

burial permit: Required by some states for human remains to be buried or cremated, the document is customarily obtained by the mortuary or crematory. One is not required for the scattering of cremated ashes.

casket: A container designed for holding human remains. It may be made of wood, metal, or fiberglass. Rarely called a coffin.

catafalque [pronounced CAT-a-falk]: The stand on which the casket rests while the deceased is lying in state and during the funeral service.

cemetery: Ground for burial, often where final aspects of the funeral ceremony or the ceremony itself are held.

codicil [pronounced COD-a-cil]: An amendment to a will that changes an original provision.

columbarium: Structure or building for urns holding cremated remains.

community property: Property acquired by a husband and wife during the course of the marriage from the earnings or efforts of either spouse while living in a state that recognizes community property. Property received by inheritance or gift is exempt.

contest: A legal challenge to or questioning the validity of a will.

cortege [pronounced cor-TEZH]: The funeral procession.

cotenancy: Ownership of property by two or more parties without survivorship rights.

cremation: A procedure using intense heat in a chamber to incinerate human remains.

crematory: A building with a furnace for the purpose of cremating human remains.

crypt: Any chamber that holds a casket and human remains. More narrowly, an individual chamber in a mausoleum.

death certificate: A document executed by a medical health professional that legally validates the deceased's death, essential for arranging interment, estate matters, and other purposes.

devise: To pass real estate under a Will.

disclaimer: The renunciation of a gift transferred by Will or trust. Gifts that have been accepted cannot be disclaimed, a critical consideration for estate or gift tax purposes, as the disclaimer of a gift is not considered a taxable event. Also known as *renunciation*.

disinter [pronounced dis-in-TER]: Synonym for *exhume*. See opposite page.

display room: A room in a funeral home set aside for selecting caskets, urns, grave liners, and other burial items.

disposition: The general term for ground burial, scattering cremains, and all other forms of placing the remains at rest.

domicile: The place where a person has his or her residence for legal purposes.

embalming: The chemical process that temporarily preserves human remains.

escheat [pronounced es-CHEAT]: The process of law in which the state takes the deceased's assets when there are no beneficiaries or heirs.

estate tax: Federal and state taxes levied on any property that is transferred at death.

eulogy: A speech at a funeral or memorial service that honors the deceased.

Executor/Executrix: Male/female designated under a Will to administer an estate.

exhume: To dig up human remains to move to another burial site or for medical or legal investigation.

fiduciary: A person having the legal and financial duty to act for the benefit of another.

funeral director: The professional who prepares the body for burial, supervises burial and other services, and maintains a funeral home for these purposes. Also called "mortician" or "undertaker."

funeral home: An establishment that provides for the care and preparation of human remains for their final resting place. Also called a "mortuary" or "funeral service provider."

funeral insurance: An insurance policy covering all costs directly related to a funeral.

funeral service: A ceremony, at which the remains are present, where the bereaved honor the deceased.

funeral spray: A bouquet of usually twenty-five or more cut flowers sent to the deceased's residence or the funeral home in tribute to the deceased.

grantor: The person who establishes a trust. Also known as a *settlor.*

grave liner: A box or receptacle made of concrete or other durable material into which the casket is placed to prevent the ground from collapsing. Most states do not require it, although most cemeteries do.

"green burial": Also called "direct burial." The process of burying a body in a biodegradable container and without embalming to help preserve the earth.

guardian: Someone who is legally responsible for the care and well-being of another person, often a minor child or incompetent adult.

heir: A person entitled to receive property under a Will or by intestacy.

holographic Will: A Will written in the testator's handwriting.

interment: The act of burying a dead body in a grave.

intestate [pronounced in-TES-tate]: Leaving behind no legal Will, as in the phrase "to die intestate."

inurnment: Placing cremation ashes in an urn.

legacy: Technically, a gift of cash under a Will, although the word now applies to any gift.

liabilities: Mortgages and other debts in an estate.

life insurance trust: A trust funded from money provided from life insurance.

living trust: A trust that has been established during the life of the grantor. Also known as an *inter vivos* (pronounced VEE-vos) trust.

living will: A legally binding document detailing the wishes of an individual concerning his or her medical care, especially with respect to life-sustaining technology and resuscitation.

lying in state: As applied to a public figure, the casket's being presented in a public place for viewing by mourners and the public.

mausoleum: A structure or building, often on cemetery grounds, which holds caskets and remains.

morgue: A facility operated by a municipality where bodies are held pending identification by next of kin and where autopsies are conducted.

mortuary: See "funeral home."

niche [pronounced NIT-ch or NEE-sh]: An individual chamber in a columbarium where an urn is placed.

nuncupative [pronounced nun-CYUP-ative]: Oral. A nuncupative Will is valid in several states if certain qualifications are met, such as made in contemplation of immediate death, said before a certain number of witnesses, and transcribed within a brief amount of time after the testator's death.

opening and closing fees: Cemetery changes for excavating and refilling a grave.

pallbearers: Individuals, whether mourners or hired help, who carry the casket.

payable-on-death, or POD: Bank accounts that transfer the assets held to the person named as beneficiary. The assets escape probate but not estate taxes.

per capita: Literally "by the head," this phrase indicates that bequests are to be distributed to a class of beneficiaries in equal shares. A Will that indicates "to my three sons per capita . . ." means that each son will receive one-third of the legacy. It is the opposite of per stirpes.

perpetual care trust funds: A certain portion of the cost of a burial plot is set aside in a trust fund for its ongoing care (usually restricted to such groundskeeping chores as lawn mowing.

personalized funeral: A nontraditional type of funeral in which the mourners create and take part in the proceedings, including preparing the deceased for burial.

per stirpes: Literally "by the branch," this phrase indicates that bequests are to be distributed according by generation. If the testator has two children and one child has two children (named A and B) and the other only one (named C), then "to my grandchildren per stirpes" means that A and B each receives 25 percent and C receives 50 percent. It is the opposite of per capita.

preneed or preplanning: Arranging all aspects of a funeral, including financing, in advance of death.

probate: The court process of proving the validity of a Will.

remains: The body of the deceased.

renunciation: See "disclaimer."

reposing room: A room of the funeral home where the body rests until the funeral service.

right of survivorship: The survivor's right to acquire joint property, an alternative to receiving the property under a Will or via intestacy and thus avoiding probate.

rigor mortis: The increased rigidity of muscles that sets in after death.

shivah [pronounced SHIV-ah]: In Judaism, the seven-day period of mourning by close relatives of the deceased, who are said to "sit shivah."

testator: The maker of a valid Will.

trust: A legal mechanism in which assets are held and managed by one person for the benefit of one or more other people.

urn: A container designed to hold cremated human remains.

vault: A solid "container," usually made of concrete, to prevent leakage from the casket into the soil.

viatical: Type of life insurance policy used before death.

vigil: In Roman Catholicism, a service held on the eve of the funeral service.

visitation: A scheduled time, usually at a funeral home, when the body is on display (if appropriate) for mourners to pay their respects.

wake: A watch over the deceased usually conducted by family members and close friends.

Will [customarily capitalized]: A legal document setting forth the intentions of the deceased concerning the dispersal of assets and such other matters as custody of minor children.

For Further Information

Chapter 1—The Event

Step by Step: Your Guide to Making Practical Decisions When a Loved One Dies by Ellen Shaw, (Quality Life Resources, 2001).

The American Association of Retired Persons—AARP— is a great source of information about a variety of end-of-life subjects. Use the search function at www.aarp.org

Chapter 2—The Funeral Home

Writing an obituary: www.wikihow.com/Write-an-Obituary; http://obituaryguide.com, http://howtowrite .weebly.com/how-to-write-an-obituary.html

Chapter 3—The Service

For a wide range of books of quotations, go to www .libraryspot.com/quotations.htm. Inspirational quotations can be found at beliefnet.com and www.inspirational-quotations. com, and poems suitable for inclusion in eulogies have been gathered in www.eulogyspeech.net/funeral-poems and www .sapphyr.net/smallgems/quotes-death.htm.

For musical suggestions, see "funeral music" at www .music-for-church-choirs.com; "funeral music" at www.buzzle .com; and www.memorialmusiclibrary.com.

For suggestions on how to create a memorial website, see "memorial website" at www.ehow.com; and for two commercial sites, go to www.sympathytree.com and www.ilasting .com. A memorial site with suggestions for other memorial sites is at www.willsworld.com/memorial.htm.

Military burials:

The Department of Veterans Affairs' National Cemetery Administration maintains 128 national cemeteries in thirty-nine states and Puerto Rico as well as thirty-three soldier's lots and monument sites. A state-by-state list is available at ww.cem.va.gov/cems/listcem.asp. Other national cemeteries in which veterans can be buried may be found through www.cem.va.gov/cems/newcem.asp. In addition, many states have established state veterans cemeteries: www.cem.va.gov/scg/lsvc.asp.

Department of Veterans Affairs regional offices will assist in determining eligibility for burial in a national cemetery. To find the nearest office, call 1-800-827-1000.

Regarding Arlington National Cemetery: www.arlingtoncemetery.org/funeral_information/index.html.

For an overview of military burials and benefits: www .military.com/benefits/burial-and-memorial.

Chapter 4—Grief Counseling and Grief Therapy

Books:

The Mourning Handbook: The Most Comprehensive Resource Offering Practical and Compassionate Advice on Coping with All Aspects of Death and Dying, by Helen Fitzgerald (Simon & Schuster/Fireside)

On Grief and Grieving: Finding the Meaning of Grief Through the Five Stages of Loss by Elisabeth Kubler-Ross with David Kessler (Scribner)

How To Go On Living When Someone You Love Dies by Therese A. Random (Bantam)

Grief Therapy (Elf Self Help) by Karen Katafiasz (Abbey Press)

No Time For Goodbyes: Coping with Sorrow, Anger, and Injustice After a Tragic Death by Janice Harris Lord (Compassion Press)

Websites:

Grief Counseling Resource Guide: www.omh.state.ny.us /omhweb/grief/#Section1

Children and Death: http://family.samhsa.gov/talk/ death.aspx and www.hospicenet.org/html/talking.html; http://kidshealth.org/parent/emotions/feelings/death .html#

Dealing with sudden death: See "sudden or traumatic death" at www.twinlesstwins.org

Dealing with tragedy: http://virginiatech.healthandperformancesolutions.net/index2.html

Chapter 5—Housekeeping

Selecting a headstone, see "choosing the right monument dealer" at www.everlifememorials.com/v/headstones

To determine other benefits involving surviving spouses and/or children, contact the SSA via its website at http:// www.ssa.gov or by phone at 1-800-772-1213.

Chapter 6—Probate: An Overview

What Is Probate: http://www.lectlaw.com/filesh/qfl08 .htm

How to Probate a Decedent's Estate:

http://www.scselfservice.org/probate/prop/Frequently AskedQuestions2.htm

State laws on probate: http://estate.findlaw.com/probate /probate-court-laws/estate-planning-law-state-probate.html

How to be an executor: search "exectutor" at www.ehow. com/how.

From the probate judge's viewpoint, see the New Mexico Judges Probate Manual at http://jec.unm.edu/resources /benchbooks/probate.

Visit www.nolo.com for a valuable and enlightening resource for all aspects of the probate process.

Chapter 7—The Probate Process

After downloading an Application for Employer Identification Number (IRS Form SS-4 at www.irs.gov), phone the IRS at (559) 452-4010 to obtain a number. The SS-4 form must be faxed to the IRS at (559) 443-6961 within twenty-four hours after the tax identification number is assigned. You must also notify the IRS of your appointment as Executor or administrator by filing a Notice of Fiduciary Relationship (IRS Form 56).

Chapter 8—Estate Planning

A specimen testamentary trust can be found by going to "sample trust" under "legal forms" at www.medlawplus.com

For state laws governing Wills, see www.nolo.com/article StateList.cfm